Hard Aground . . . Again

Inspiration for the Navigationally Challenged and Spiritually Stuck

Eddie Jones

with foreword by Ted Brewer

WILMINGTON, NORTH CAROLINA
Winoca Press

Hard Aground . . . Again: Inspiration for the Navigationally Challenged and Spiritually Stuck copyright © 2007 by Eddie Jones

Published by Winoca Press
106 North 16th Street, Wilmington, NC 28401-3819 USA
www.winocapress.com

Available direct from the publisher, from your local bookstore, or from the author at
www.hardaground.com

Printed in the United States of America
09 08 07   5 4 3 2 1

LIBRARY OF CONGRESS CATALOGING-IN-PUBLICATION DATA

Jones, Eddie, 1957–
    Hard aground—again : inspiration for the navigationally challenged and
spiritually stuck / Eddie Jones; with foreword by Ted Brewer.
      p. cm.
    ISBN-13: 978-0-9755910-9-3
    ISBN-10: 0-9755910-9-6
    1. Christian life. 2. Spiritual life. 3. Sailing. 4. Jones, Eddie, 1957–   I. Title.
BV4501.3.J644 2006
242´.68—dc22

                                                                        2006033481

Book cover designed by Eddie Jones; interior designed by Barbara Brannon
Illustrations by Mel Neale and Melanie Neale
"A Prayer to Follow Jesus" is used with permission of Dr. Gregory P. Rogers.
Scriptures are quoted from the New International Version of the Bible.

When daylight came, they did not recognize the land, but they saw a bay with a sandy beach. The ship, however, struck a sandbar and ran aground. The bow stuck fast and would not move, and the stern was broken to pieces by the pounding of the surf.

—Paraphrased from the account of Paul's voyage to Rome in Acts 27

The secret to life
is enjoying the passage
of the tides!

Dedication

My father died during the writing of this book, but I've been writing this book for almost a decade so I can't blame him for not waiting around to see its completion. My dad was a patient man, but not that patient.

My dad loved fishing. He could sit in a chair on the beach all day waiting for a strike. He'd wait and watch and then pull them in, sometimes two fish at a time. Then he'd bait his hooks, cast the line beyond the breakers, and go back to waiting. I think that's why he was so patient with me. He was waiting to catch me. Waiting for me to love him the way he loved me. I do now, Dad.

He tried to teach me to hunt once. We walked down to the Neuse River on a cool fall afternoon and sat on a log. He told me to sit still and be quiet. I did — for about five minutes. Then I picked up acorns and began trying to hit a tree. He let this go on for a while and then asked me to stop. I did. A few minutes later I found a stick and began snapping it into smaller pieces. He didn't say anything. He just waited until I had a good pile of kindling between my legs. But when I picked up another stick, he asked me to stop. I did. I found if I burrowed my boots into the soil I could make some really deep holes under the leaves. I began this project next but Dad looked over at me and asked if I was finished hunting, if I'd had a good time and was ready to go home. I said I was. That was the last time Dad took me hunting, but it wasn't the last time we went off in the woods together.

My dad used to take me camping in the Great Smoky Mountains. It always rained when we went, which was good since the rain kept the black bears away. But sometimes it didn't rain hard enough and the bears visited our tent anyway. Dad always understood when we wanted to sleep in the Volkswagen instead of the tent. Dad and the bears got along just fine, though. Dad was like that. He could tolerate almost anyone, including my mom for over fifty years.

So this book is dedicated to my dad, Raymond Jones, because during all those years when he was trying to teach me to fish, hunt, camp, work on motors, and hit a baseball he never gave up on me. He always figured one day I'd get it, figure out what I was good at and do it well in the same way he learned to fish and hunt and camp and be a dad. The writer of Proverbs says: "Train a child in the way he should go, and when he is old he will not turn from it." My dad knew long ago I'd need lots of patience as I learned to love, feed my family, and fight for my dreams as I ran aground on the shoals of life. So he gave me the gift of patience by being patient with me.

That's what dads do best. Thanks, Dad. ➤

Contents

Foreword   Ted Brewer

I WAS FIRST INTRODUCED TO EDDIE JONES'S UNIQUE BRAND OF HUMOR in the pages of the late, lamented *Coastal Cruising* magazine. What first caught my eye was the photo of Eddie enjoying a cool brew while relaxing (loafing?) in the cockpit of one of my Nimble 20 sailboats. Like any proud papa I immediately recognized the boat as one of my offspring and, not being averse to a cool one myself, it intrigued me. So, naturally, I had to read that article, and once I did I was hooked. I continued to enjoy Eddie's offbeat humor and quixotic tales in *Coastal Cruising* as long as the magazine kept arriving in my mail.

Being an avid Eddie Jones fan by then, when I saw an ad for his first book, *Hard Aground with Eddie Jones,* I couldn't wait to place my order. The day the package arrived from the publisher I tore it open, sat down, and read that little book through cover to cover in one evening. I was rewarded with many a hearty laugh, and even more chuckles, as I devoured the slim volume. So very many of Eddie's stories reminded me of dumb mistakes I'd made or some fool thing that either happened to me, or to someone I know. History does repeat itself!

As a result, I jumped at the chance when Eddie asked if I'd write a foreword for his new book, *Hard Aground . . . Again,* and I was not disappointed when I read the proof drafts that he e-mailed. There is a satisfyingly large dose of Eddie's down-to-earth humor in the book, along with a goodly supply of advice (some of it actually useful!). To my surprise, Eddie also illustrates the stories and the advice with pithy verses from the Bible. While not deeply religious myself, I still found these scriptural quotes to be interesting, enlightening and, often, inspiring.

If you enjoy maritime humor you will enjoy *Hard Aground . . . Again.* You may even learn something from it, but I wouldn't guarantee that. I will guarantee that you'll have many a good laugh, usually at Eddie's expense, and you might even see yourself reflected in some of his wacky anecdotes. ➤

Acknowledgments

THIS IS THE PART OF THE BOOK THAT PEOPLE SKIM TO SEE IF THEIR NAME is included. Unless you loaned me money, gave me a boat, or paid me to write in your publication then your name's probably not here, so you can move on to the next page, which features a detailed analysis of Dan Brown's DNA that proves without a doubt that he descended from a turnip. Did I say Dan Brown? I meant Dan Quall. If you *did* loan me money and are still waiting to get paid — or if your name's Dan — then all I can say is, "What were you thinking?"

First I'd like to thank Keith for *not* changing his last name to Penkava when he married Melinda. Spelling Keith Smith is hard enough. I'd also like to thank Keith for giving my "Hard Aground" column a home on TownDock.net. We had some good laughs in those early years before Oriental grew up to forty-eight and a half feet.

Thanks to Norm at Bay River Pottery for giving me a boat.

Thanks to John Farmer at Camp Don Lee for allowing me to pilfer parts from the abandoned boats in his canoe creek. Methodists are kind in that way.

Thanks to Kevin Spencer for sending ten dollars so he could advertise on *Shoal Survivor*'s toilet seat. I think about you a lot, Kevin. Okay, that didn't sound right, so let's move on.

Thanks to Terry Whalin for helping me write a nonfiction book proposal. If your book project has been rejected more times than an Israeli Palestinian peace plan then buy Terry's *Book Proposals That Sell: 21 Secrets To Speed Your Success* and you too might become a poor but published author someday.

Thanks to Bert Quay, former editor of *Carolina Cruising* magazine, for giving me a start as a boating columnist. We sure showed them, didn't we?

Thanks to Knute for letting me stay in Slip None on the North Dock of Whittaker Creek for free. Sorry about the stench of my boat. Stink happens.

Thanks to Ted Jones at *Coastal Cruising* for helping me become a better writer — and for actually giving me money and praise for my column.

Thanks to Dave and Carolyn Corbett for letting me spear lobsters under *Bifrost*. Too bad the marriage didn't work out. It was a nice boat.

Thanks to Tom Neale for running my Hard Aground column in *Cruising Coast and Islands*. Sorry I ruined your publication. Thanks to Tom's wife, Mel, for the cover artwork, and to their daughter, Melanie, for the inside illustrations. I'm sure the readers will agree the pretty pictures are the best part of the book.

Thanks to Pat Patterson for fixing the things I break on my boat. We make a great team. Thanks also to Dan Boney for giving me new boats and motors for Pat to repair.

Thanks to Dave and Jaja Martin for encouraging me to leave the slip and see the world from the deck of a sailboat. And for demonstrating the importance of birth control.

Thanks to Ted Brewer, Greg Rogers, Barbara Brannon, Al Gansky, and my wife, Bennie, for their help with this book. I could have done it without you, but how stupid would that have been? ➤

Prologue

Missing the Boat

I CAN REMEMBER THE EXACT MOMENT I DECIDED TO DITCH MY TRIMARAN. We were motoring down the channel to Whittaker Creek after a turbulent passage back from Beaufort. My friend Tina was basking in the sun on a beach towel, her head resting on a mildew-stained seat cushion positioned at the base of the mast. My sister and her boyfriend were sitting in lounge chairs on the bow waving at the skipper of the towboat. I was standing in the cockpit with my hand on the tiller, looking east towards the dinghy beach, hoping this would be the last time I steered that sorry sailboat back to its slip.

I'd had enough of that boat.

The thumbnail of sand wrapping around the curve of the dinghy beach was wide and white, as it had been so many other days when my sons and I had collected an assortment of buried treasure and bug bites. Those had been good days fashioned into fond memories, but they were at least two boats ago and now my boys were driving and shaving and no longer interested in exploring the dinghy beach — or any other stretch of shoreline — if it meant spending another night aboard that trimaran. I studied the curb of sand at the water's edge that had been our imaginary pirate's paradise, and my heart ached to admit that I had squandered five years of their youth on a boat-building project that had soured their love for sailing.

I was sick of that boat.

I was still looking towards the dinghy beach when my sister stood from her lounge chair and hollered across the cabin.

"He wants to know which slip is yours."

"North Dock," I shouted over the roar of the towboat's engine. "Just tell him to take us to North Dock."

The skipper of the towboat throttled down as he rounded the last marker, allowing the line to our bow to go slack before reeling us in. I pointed up the creek and we surged forward, continuing our journey back to Slip None. This final passage had begun six hours earlier when I had lost my last good outboard and second motor in two days to a series of bad decisions. A BoatUS towboat operator had found us drifting with the tide at the base of the Grayden Paul Bridge in Beaufort, North Carolina, and so, as I had done so many times before, I was being led back to port in the wake of a towboat.

I was finished with that boat.

I had bought *Kontigo* on a whim. It had been sitting across the dock from our Ranger 23 and my two boys had convinced me that it was just the kind of boat our family needed. It sailed flat, was cheap, and had more character than a whole fleet of Beneteaus. I remember the evening my wife and I considered making an offer to purchase it.

"If we buy that old trimaran we had better learn to love everything about it because there's no way we'll ever be able to sell it," I'd explained to the boys. "It's just too odd and ugly." But I was wrong. It turns out there was at least one other couple that liked our odd-looking trimaran and by the grace of God they found us. But that would be a year later. A year after my final passage on *Kontigo*. A year after I gave up on my dream.

I was finished with cruising.

"Beauty and affliction are the only two things that pierce the human heart," Simone Weil says, and my passion for sailing had left me vulnerable to both. I had seen the sands of Cape Lookout sparkle white as sugar as a cool northeast wind swept across the point. I had seen the shallow waters off the beach fade from teal to cobalt and felt the warmth of the sun on my face as I lay on the deck of that boat.

To love is to lose because we cannot hold onto the things we love. Not the beauty of a sunset, not the laughter of our children, not the life of our spouse. Our time on earth passes quickly, but thank God this life is not the real meal. It is just a sampling, a smorgasbord of the heavenly banquet that awaits those who have responded in the affirmative to his invitation. When we snack on the meager rations we're issued and believe that is the feast, we miss the point. Beauty is a gift we cannot keep. Affliction is the curse that does not last. And both drive us into the arms of God. Cruising with that trimaran had led me closer to God because my prayers for relief had become intense.

So I sold the boat on a whim, of sorts, to a couple from the West Coast. We had scheduled the sea trial for a Sunday afternoon that called for fair skies and light winds, but when they arrived to test-drive the boat a small gale was brewing off the coast. Since I no longer owned an outboard, I had hoped to sail the boat from and back to the dock but with the deteriorating weather that was no longer possible, so I commandeered a friend's four-horsepower Johnson. It was hardly the right tool for the job but it was all we had.

I was about to suggest we reschedule the sea trial for another day when Wym stepped aboard. He looked across the cabin and his eyes sparkled as he felt for the hand of his bride. I watched the wrinkles on his face fade as his smile widened. He was anxious for the boat to depart. Anxious for his dream to begin. Anxious to take his bride on a boat ride.

This couple had a love for my boat that I lost long ago, and time was running out on their dream too. Wym had just turned eighty and Gail was in her mid-sixties. They would have only a few months to prepare the boat before embarking on their first winter cruise to the Keys.

I explained that we might not be able to leave the creek due to the strong winds and the fact that *Kontigo* motored into the wind like a dock box towing a crab pot. They nodded, as if being polite, and then asked if they could untie the dock lines. As Gail tossed the bowline onto the fuel dock the wind stopped. It was as if someone had unplugged a very large fan blowing in my face.

There was nothing left to do but trust God, so I motored out the creek, down the channel, and into the Neuse River. We made better speed than expected given the size of the channel chop, and when we reached the final marker the wind returned, providing a broad reach across the river. Wym and Gail were still smiling, still holding hands, still waiting for the sail they'd been promised — so I hoisted the main and relaxed as *Kontigo* surged forward the way she had years before when she and I were still in love. I passed the tiller to Gail and then carried my lounge chair to the bow for the final time. I already knew, without being told, that *Kontigo* had passed her final test.

I was looking towards the village of Oriental when a little of the brown "Neuse juice" splashed up through the netting of the trampoline and onto my bare feet, cooling my toes and warming my heart. I began to reflect on all the hard work we'd put into this boat — the tinted windows my oldest son, Win, had helped install, the galley sink Mason had found in the trash heap, the bunks in the salon my buddy Pat had built from a set of plans he'd scribbled on a napkin at M & M's. Those had been fun times and some great memories. Suddenly a flood of tears welled up in my eyes, washing away the pain of disappointment and leaving only wonderful memories of days spent working and sailing with family and friends on an old boat that I'd thought I'd keep forever.

God, I'm gonna miss that boat.

▷ ▷ ▷

You probably gather by now that when I sold my old trimaran I did not give up the dream. At least, not all the way. I'm in phase five of a twelve-step program that my probation officer (my wife) hopes will cure my addiction to boats, sailing, and sandbar hopping. Right now I'm learning to ride a Jet Ski and race around no-wake buoys. Next week I'm going to buy a used Bayliner. By the time I reach step twelve — the rank of yacht broker — I'm certain I'll never want to own a boat again.

But until they release me from "the home" I have to face the fact that I'm a recovering boataholic. I wish cruising wasn't my passion. I wish I loved golf or bowling or cooking, but I didn't choose this affliction. It picked me. There isn't a cure for people like us. There's only tough love, because you have to be tough to love a dream that continues to break your heart. That's why I wrote this book. It's a love story between a God who places the call of the sea in our heart and our desperate need to see his world from the deck of a sailboat. It's a motivational guide for those who long to get their life unstuck and their dreams soaring again.

Perhaps long ago you were going to quit your job and sail to the islands. You went to the cruising seminars and listened to Tom and Mel, Dave and Jaja, or Doug and Bernadette. You schemed and dreamed, and then bought the boat. But somewhere between that first time you wrapped the dock line around the propeller and that final family vacation you spent navigating It's a Small World at Disneyland you ran aground on the shoals of family, finances, or failing health. You gave up on the dream, and now you're stuck or worse. You've come to accept life in the mud. Well, take heart.

Noah had a hundred years to plan his first cruise and he still ran aground at the end of the passage. The Apostle Paul dreamed of harbor-hopping the coast of Italy but wrecked on a reef and had to swim ashore. Even the great and powerful Moses got stuck in the weeds of the Nile. Running aground is nothing to be ashamed of, but staying stuck is.

In the pages that follow you will learn how to enjoy a good grounding, gain discernment from disappointments, and laugh at your mistakes. Each essay begins with a Ha-Ha moment — a Hard Aground Heart Ache — followed by a life application, a supporting scripture, and a bit of wisdom. There is also a prayer focus for those who believe in that sort of thing. I do. Sandbar hopping has taught me to pray in ways that church never could. So if your dreams are stuck and you are wondering if God is faithful, remember this: Noah didn't have charts, GPS, channel markers, or guidebooks, and God called him to the sea.

Perhaps he is calling you, too. ▷

Hard Aground
. . . Again

A sailboat is a lousy place to hold an argument because you can slam a hatch board in place only so hard, and it never has the same effect as banging a door shut. Women always get the main cabin after a fight, which leaves us men in the cockpit with the rain and bugs. You can see why men will go to almost any extreme, including jumping ship, to avoid an argument.

Part I

Anchors Away: Basic Seamanship Gone Awry

1

Think Globally, Sail Locally

LIFE IS SO HECTIC THESE DAYS THAT IT'S HARD TO TELL IF I'M COMING or going. In fact, yesterday I got so turned around that I passed myself on the docks. It wasn't me exactly, but it could've been. We were like two ships passing in the night, that skinny guy and I.

My wife and I were reclining in the cockpit of a Crealock 37, talking with our yacht broker about staterooms and headroom and monthly cash flow. I say "our yacht broker" because we've shelled out so much money at his establishment that I feel as if we ought to have some ownership papers on him. He says we're the cheapest occupants he's ever had, and that we've gotten off light considering what most people pay for his dockage, fuel, and maintenance services. It's the nature of marina moguls like him to say these things.

It was the sight of the skinny man leading his kids and pregnant wife down the docks that set my mind to wandering south towards the Bahamas — that, and the strong aroma of stale bilge water mixed with diesel fumes. It's an odd combination, I admit, but boat odors are an intoxicating elixir for me. The attraction to diesel fumes goes back to my grandfather's tractor and the wide-open spaces of his farm in Pender County. Acres of prime tobacco and the stale sweat of cousins and field hands plucking leaves is just the sort of pasture to set a young mind to cultivating a need to be any place other than where you are.

1

The Crealock's bilge odor reminded me of that first night in Hopetown Harbour. It was there that I discovered just how infectious cruising could be. I'd been invited to spend a week sailing around the Abacos and soon found myself wondering why everyone didn't do this. I've since learned that money, marriage, and mortgages can cripple the dream, but I didn't know this that first night as I lay in my bunk savoring the distinct smell of diesel. I thought that buying a boat and cruising the islands was something everyone could do.

So as I sat in the cockpit of that Crealock 37 contemplating a winter in the Bahamas, that skinny man with his family of three and a half reminded me that he had already seen more wide open beaches and spent more nights at sea than I could imagine, and he'd done it all on a boat almost half of the size of the one my wife and I were casing.

I don't mind telling you it's pretty frustrating to have two boys and a wife racing after every suburban seduction society can offer except for the one diversion I keep pushing at them. I can see my life's ambition slipping away even as others assure me that it will all work out in the end.

"Just be patient," they say. "Your time will come." That's what they said about my friend Tom, too, and when his time came it arrived with a mass of malignant tumors and some veiled lie about remission. We buried Tom a few months later. Some days your time comes for all the wrong reasons.

That's why I had my family down at the marina that fall afternoon. I was lobbying my constituents for a little PAC-it-up money and a boat to blow it on. For those who don't know us well or haven't seen us aground along the Waterway, allow me to introduce you to the Joneses. We're a lively brood, so try and keep up.

On the foredeck we have Bennie, my wife and the homemaker in our family. College-educated and graduated with honors, Bennie comes from good stock. This is a polite way of saying that none of her immediate family has been locked up for longer than a weekend, been institutionalized for a mental disorder, or graduated from the University of North Carolina. Half her clan comes from the hollows and foothills of the Appalachian Mountains and, contrary to local lore, not everyone up there is a kissing cousin, sister, or brother.

In fact, not too long ago Bennie's brother married a fine Yankee woman from Pennsylvania, so it's not like Bennie's the only one to bring shame to her family by marrying outside the clan.

On the helm we have Win, our oldest, and it's because of him that we sold our old Ranger 33 sailboat. I don't mean that we rearranged our whole life to suit our oldest boy, but Win has a gift and a dream, and sailing in May, June, and July are not part of his program. He has a knack for hitting a baseball and he's a very determined ball player who truly loves the game. Like so many boys his age, he's struggling to understand why the bigger kids who play prefer mid-season strikes to hits and runs. The lessons on greed come later in life — high school, I think it is.

When asked on job applications where I see myself in ten years, I reply, "Sailing around the world, writing a best-selling novel, and surfing the best reef breaks." I rarely get called back for a second interview. Ask Win this question and he says, "On my way to breaking Hank Aaron's home-run record." He's caught sight of the highest peak in his small world and the ascent has begun. Far be it from me to scatter sharp stones along his path. My hope is that I can talk him into playing for a team whose ballpark is within biking distance of a marina. My first choice is the Orioles, because then we can sail the Chesapeake on his days off, but Seattle would be nice too.

Mason is our youngest, and the world is his playground. Actually the world and our neighbors' backyard — or any yard. It doesn't matter. Mason's not shy about welcoming himself into your life. He's the one I send down the dock to borrow a ratchet set from a slipmate because I'm too cheap to buy one myself. Between church, Scouts, school activities, and ballgames, we Joneses set a blistering pace around here. Compared to us, the Martins seem frozen in place.

Dave Martin orbits the globe at sea level, moving through life at hull speed. He's seen the volcano peaks I dream of and lived through the storms I fear, so while Bennie and I were bickering over the proper size of a cruising sailboat, our yacht broker suggested I talk with Dave and Jaja. With their third child due that January, they were doubling up the spring lines and looking forward to spending the winter in Oriental.

"I'm ready to be any place cooler than Florida," Dave said. "We're tired of the heat."

"You'll like Oriental," I offered. "Things are quiet and definitely not hot in the winter. Do you plan on keeping *Direction* after your third child arrives?"

"It'll be cramped. With Chris and Holly growing up so fast, it already is."

"I know the feeling. I had a Nimble 20 that was fine for weekend sailing but it shrank when our second son arrived. We just didn't have any place to store all those messy diapers."

"Yeah, we have to get ready for that all over again. Jaja and I are already looking for a little larger boat, but there's so much junk floating in the ocean that I'm partial to steel. It's harder to sink."

"Well, I'm trying to sell my family on heading to the Bahamas next year, so any boat larger than the last one we had is fine with me."

"You'll like it in the Bahamas," he said. "We did."

Yes, I could tell. Any couple that marries and raises a family on the ocean would like a place with wide-open spaces and a casual culture. The question is, would Chris and Holly have liked it as much if they'd begun their adventure in America's suburbs? Will Mason and Win like it better than baseball, Scouts, and the backyard freedom of their suburban America? Each course has its tradeoffs. Anything worthwhile does. Like watching your son grow into a man on a midnight watch in the middle of the Atlantic, instead of watching him start second base in his first All-Star game. Like shooting basketball with your boys in the driveway instead of shooting lobster on the reef in the Abacos. Who's to say for certain which is the better course to chart? Only God knows, and most days he's not telling. At least not with words I can understand.

But that doesn't mean he's not speaking. Oftentimes the passions that pre-occupy my mind, the desires that shape my dreams, are the gentle proddings of an almighty God. I've found that nothing of value is ever created without desire. It is the very fabric of who we are. If you want to know what you were meant to do, look within at what you want to do. Unless it's something that controls you, makes others stumble, or leads you to sin, then chances are it is worthy of your time and God's blessing. And if it leads you to praise God and tell others about his goodness, then it is absolutely a course worth pursuing.

Our dreams and passions are the fuel that allow us to serve others. We are called to be the feet of Christ, carrying the good news to others. We are called to be his hands, ministering to those in need. If God has put a passion for sailing in your heart and placed people in need along your route, then it's time to get on with the passage.

➤ **Hard Aground hint:** You are free to choose the passage, but you are not free from the storms of that passage. The rain will come, but so too will the rainbow and both are blessings from God.

➤ **Passage markers:** *Each one should use whatever gift he has received to serve others, faithfully administering God's grace in its various forms.* —I Peter 4:10. For further inspiration read Luke 18:15–17.

➤ **Prayer focus:** Those who know in their heart what God is calling them to do, but are afraid to act.

2

A Stern Response to a Heated Discussion

To all my friends — both of them — who have, over the years, chided me for squandering my money on sailboats and surf wax when I could have been investing six percent of my income in a company-sponsored retirement account, I have just three words: Enron, WorldCom, and I can't recall the other one but I think it has something to do with crossing the ocean in a small boat. Before I continue boasting about how smart I was to buy a thirty-year-old sailboat while everyone else was investing in the dot-com collapse, I have this disturbing news to report from St. Thomas.

It seems a man leapt to safety Tuesday from the eighth deck of a cruise ship as it was departing Charlotte Amalie harbor. Eyewitness accounts indicate that at around eight p.m., as the ship passed Marriott's Frenchman's Reef Beach Resort on its way out of the harbor, a thirty-nine-year-old man flung himself over the banister of the top deck and executed a perfect cannonball buster. A Port Arthur pilot whale rescued the man and his shredded trunks.

No, wait. What I meant to say was that a Port Authority pilot boat rescued the man. Forget the whale part. Initial reports indicate that someone telephoned the cruise ship around 5:30 p.m. to say that a "device" had been placed aboard the vessel. According to a spokesman for the cruise ship, the captain ordered the vessel evacuated, but no threatening device was found, so the passengers were allowed to reboard. It wasn't until later that evening, as the ship was leaving the harbor, that the man jumped.

At first I thought the man had really slow reflexes, but I later learned that he and his wife had been quarrelling over who was the real brains behind the evening's entertainment, Tony Orlando or Dawn. It was apparently this disagreement, and not the "device," which caused him to jump.

Now at this point I have to ask the obvious. What was he thinking? Of course Dawn was the brains behind the band. And someone should tell the guy that jumping from a cruise ship is a terrible way to end an argument. If you want to jump ship, pick a smaller boat, dude. Whenever my wife and I argue, I almost always dive off the back of my boat. No, wait. Bennie and I never argue, so strike that part. What I meant to say was, *if* Bennie and I ever argued, I would jump off the back of my boat.

A sailboat is a lousy place to hold an argument because you can slam a hatch board in place only so hard, and it never has the same effect as banging a door shut. Women always get the main cabin after a fight, which leaves us men in the cockpit with the rain and bugs. You can see why men will go to almost any extreme, including jumping ship, to avoid an argument.

On our boat, we have a temperamental thermostat — and my wife is the oral thermometer. When she's not happy, nobody's happy, and most days she's not happy with me. I think she blames God for this, but I remind her that God's doing the best he can with what he has to work with. Sometimes, in a loving, biblical way, I'll make a comment about some of her character deficiencies, but apparently the scripture verse that says "An honest answer is like a kiss on the lips" wasn't meant as advice for husbands.

That's why I've developed a list of tips to help reduce onboard misunderstandings. These hints were lifted from conversations I've had with other men floating around the anchorage at dusk, slapping mosquitoes and watching for dorsal fins. I don't know if any of these tips work since I've never actually used any of them, but I might try one or two the next time my wife is in a good mood. I think the third Tuesday of the eighth month is that day this year. Anyway, here are some of the ways you and your mate can avoid the misunderstandings that lead to a stern conversation.

- If something we say can be interpreted two ways and one of the ways makes you sad or angry, then we meant the other one.
- When it's time to go ashore, absolutely anything a woman wears or doesn't wear is fine. Really.
- Christopher Columbus didn't need directions, and neither do we. We got you this far, didn't we?
- Learn to work the toilet in the head. Flush as you go and use small amounts of toilet paper. It's not a landfill.
- Ask for what you want. Let us be clear on this one. Subtle hints do not work. Strong hints do not work. Obvious hints do not work. Just say what you want and be done with it.
- We don't remember dates and can barely remember our own names, so mark birthdays and anniversaries on a calendar and remind us often.
- Our "Yes" and "No" are interchangeable answers and perfectly acceptable for almost every question.
- If it itches, we're going to scratch it, so look the other way.
- Come to us with a problem only if you want help solving it.
- If you think you're fat, you are, so don't ask.

• And when it comes to our own appearance, we are in shape. Round is a shape.

I have no idea what my wife wants from me, but I have a hunch it has something to do with spending long hours at a shopping mall, passing long evenings on a cruise ship, or being cherished and treated with gentleness. But as I said, this is just a guess, because when she gave me her top ten list of ways we could avoid onboard misunderstandings I wasn't paying attention.

So what, if anything, can we learn from our buddy's desperate attempt to escape another argument with his wife? First, it is possible to splash the promenade deck if you hit the water with enough velocity and butt mass. Second, pilot whales and pilot boats look a lot alike, but are really two distinct species that have a history of saving husbands and prophets from the sea when they have lost an argument with their wife or God. One smells like dead fish and aftershave, so if you have a choice, go with the pilot whale. Third . . . I forgot the third point, but I did remember that other thing.

If you're going to invest six percent of your income in a company called Global Crossing, make sure they're into fiberglass, not fiber optics, and if they're not, use the money to buy your own boat and go global crossing yourself. Then if your investment goes belly-up and you have to jump ship, you'll know who to blame.

But even if you forget who's at fault, it's a sure bet your wife will help you remember.

➤ **Hard Aground hint:** *Better to live in a desert than with a quarrelsome and ill-tempered wife.* —Proverbs 21:19

➤ **Passage markers:** *Better to live on a corner of the roof than share a house with a quarrelsome wife.* —Proverbs 21:9. For further inspiration read Proverbs 27:15–16.

➤ **Prayer focus:** Couples struggling to adjust to diverse personalities, desires, and dreams.

3

The Haves and the Half-Knots

YACHTING, AS YOU KNOW, WAS ORIGINALLY INTENDED FOR WEALTHY New England robber barons who made their fortunes in shipping, railroads, and tax evasion, but today it's open to anybody who can pillage, plunder, and buy a Hunter sailboat. It was William Vanderbilt, I think, who said if you have to ask the price of a yacht then you can't afford it. When I got my first sailboat I couldn't afford it. I knew it, but I bought it anyway. Since then I've consumed five sailboats and I'm working on a sixth, but the fact is I can't afford this boat or any boat at any price. It's guys like me who give yachting a bad name, but that's what happens when you offer instant credit at boat shows.

Speaking of bad names, it was William's grandfather Cornelius who changed his name to "Commodore" Vanderbilt, thus introducing the tradition of adding exotic nicknames linked to a man's vocation or vacation. Because of this, guys like Henry Morgan became known as Cap'n Morgan, Victor Bergeron became Trader Vic, and men working in factories and cubicles across America became known in the break room as "Skip." Skip offers the possibility for advancement and adventure that Milton never can.

But never mind all that. What we're discussing today is the Haves and the Half-Knots and how Commodore Vanderbilt's grandson, Billy, made a name for himself during the Depression while the rest of the country struggled to find enough beer to feed the Irish. Yachting offered Billy everything his inherited millions couldn't: shame, fear, and death by drowning. Billy forged a

reputation as an outstanding yachtsman and became known in sailing circles
— today we call this a racecourse — as Billy Kissam My Stern Vanderbilt, in
part because of his ruthless tactics, but mostly because Billy Kissam was his real
name. Billy could win any regatta on any boat against any opponent. Offspring
of other industrial tycoons knew this and steered clear of him at the starting
line. Often, as a sign of their great respect, they didn't even invite him to the
race.

Well, I don't share in Billy's wealth or talent, but my navigational skills do
strike terror in the hearts of others, so I'm often uninvited to gatherings where
boats, bars, and boorish behavior are present. When it comes to the Haves and
Half-Knots, I'm the half-wit who's left out. But that's what happens when you
keep an old sailboat in the middle of a shallow creek and fail to make your
mortgage payments on time. People and time tend to pass you by.

But staying out of the mainstream, whether in society or sailing, has
its advantages. To the casual observer strolling down East Dock in Oriental,
North Carolina, my yacht appears quaint anchored in the middle of Whittaker
Creek. Life is simple out here on the hook and it shows. Nobody walks by my
boat at six in the morning coughing their fool head off, and I no longer suffer
from the bedlam of dock carts loaded with groceries, luggage, and kids banging over a trestle of broken planks. There's almost always a breeze out here in
the creek, keeping the bugs and heat at bay during the balmy summer months.
I rarely motor back to my mooring. Instead, I sail up the creek, dousing the jib
as I slide to a stop. I play my tunes loud and belch whenever I please, and no
one seems to mind except my wife, who forgives my petty indulgences because
she can now shower and dress without wondering if someone is staring into
her cabin from the dock. All in all, life is less complicated out here in the creek.
Tranquility is what you see. Cheap is what I am. It costs more to stay at the
dock. Almost as much as my boat payment.

We don't have refrigeration on my boat. Instead, we have a poorly insu-
lated icebox tucked in a corner of the galley that is too close to the engine to
keep anything cool other than my wife's appetite for cruising. I know friends
who have refrigeration and they run their engines a lot. It must take a lot of
amps to keep a six-pack of soft drinks and cold cuts chilled. Often these friends

will offer us steaks and chicken because their weeklong cruising plans were cut short by refrigeration problems. This makes me think that all refrigeration units come equipped with a cooling coil linked to the knot log that gets tripped when the distance from dock and degrees Fahrenheit reach a set number pre-calibrated at the factory. This defrosting feature shuts down the unit, leaving everything to rot — including your family's desire to go cruising. One thing you can say about block ice. It's cold till it's gone, and then it's time to buy some more.

My Ranger 33 sailboat is over twenty years old, and as you might expect from a sea-sunned senior, she likes things the old-fashioned way. Take her headsail, for instance. She prefers the hanked-on look to the roller and furls style. We keep three outfits on board. A grand, flowing smock from Genoa, Italy, a modest working uniform for those twenty-knot days, and finally a skimpy little number that she hardly ever wears and that barely covers her forestay.

Occasionally I'll change her attire during a long passage, but not often. She's usually content with the first outfit I select. If she blows a seam or tears a hem it takes only a few moments to swap out skirts before we're back on our way again. Try clearing a jammed furling drum from a pitching bow and you'll soon long for the simplicity of hanked-on sails.

Entertainment on board is a $39.95 boom box from Radio Shack. It plays CDs, picks up AM radio stations offshore, and runs on an adapter plugged into the cigarette lighter. It's not sophisticated, but it's easy to install and easier to re-place when sea spray coats the circuit board with salt. An elaborate entertain-ment unit installed behind a recessed bulkhead and fitted with Bose speakers might sound great, but I'm no electrical engineer. I've touched a few live wires — I'm speaking of the copper strand type, not the copper-haired ones — so I know electricity works. I just don't know how it works. What I do know is that it's silent, it's invisible, and it can kill you at the right voltage, so I tend to leave it alone. This is good advice for the redheads, too.

We don't have a hot-water heater on board, just a hot engine, so if we have hot water it only lasts as long as the engine's running. When we have hot water we don't have cold, so our showers are either too hot or too cold, but

they're always uncomfortable. Sometimes we use the sun shower. The boys and I like this simple approach, but I've noticed that other boaters take offense to our communal bathing, so I wouldn't recommend this practice. Given all the things I say in print, I'm always in hot water anyway, so a water heater would only be redundant.

We've never owned a boat with an alcohol stove that worked, and the one that came with this boat isn't functional either. I like the convenience of propane, but not the work and engineering required to build a home for the tanks, so we have a $42.50 propane camping stove for our boat. It's fast, it's hot, and it works every time. Oh, sure, there is the slight possibility that one of the canisters might leak fumes into the bilge and blow us to Beaufort, but if it does, you won't hear me complain about it again.

Our navigation station includes old charts, dividers, and a yellow legal pad with heading and estimated speed entered on the hour from previous passages. My wife says I don't need anything more elaborate. "GPS would only tempt you to go someplace you have no business going," Bennie says, "so if we can't turn left and hit land by dark, then I'm not going."

I guess what I'm saying is that I'm grateful for the "yacht" that I have. I have to be. It's all I can't afford. The fact is, if I had something larger and nicer with the condo comforts of other yachts I might be tempted to stay on the hook, feasting on crackers and cheese while the rest of the world sailed in and out of our marina. Poverty motivates me in ways prosperity never could. It pushes me to dream big, hope large, and leave the navigation to the one who created the shallow waters. When, during those quite moments of despair, I reflect on the desires God has placed in my heart, I know that I was designed for more than the small adventures I've enjoyed.

Dreams, hopes, and desires are the essence of the human soul. They are the fuel that launches us out of bed and into another dull day. Absolutely nothing of human greatness is ever achieved without them. Not a business. Not a ministry. Not a marriage. Sometimes you must want something badly and be willing to work for it — often for many years — before God wants it for you too.

The Psalmist encourages us all with a hopeful promise: "Delight yourself in the Lord and he will give you the desires of your heart." Only when we delight in God is it safe for him to give us our desires, because then the fuel of our passions will then become the necessary energy to serve him. Saint Augustine said, "The whole life of the good Christian is a holy longing. What you desire ardently, as yet you do not see. So, let us long because we are to be filled. That is our life, to be exercised by longing." As you can see, Saint Augustine had a funny way of saying things, but then he was busy building a beach in Florida and probably didn't write everything he wrote.

The great enemy of God's kingdom is not sin — it's contentment. We desire to be entertained instead of engaged. We seek amusement, instead of amazement at what God wants for us. We settle for the small things, thinking that's all God wants for us. But it never is. He gave us his son that we might have life and have it abundantly. This is not a guarantee of material prosperity. But it is a promise that he will bless us abundantly with the currency of his choosing when we work within his will.

When viewed in this way, then it's clear that what separates the Haves from the Half-Knots is not prosperity and poverty, but the size of your dreams and your willingness to follow God . . . wherever that calling leads you. When seen in that light, we can all be rich indeed.

➤ **Hard Aground hint:** "To suppose . . . that we could be rich and not behave as the rich behave, is like supposing that we could drink all day and keep absolutely sober." —LOGAN PEARSALL SMITH

➤ **Passage markers:** *The Lord will fulfill his purpose for me; your love, O Lord, endures forever — do not abandon the works of your hands.* —Psalm 138:8. For further inspiration read I Kings 17:1–15.

➤ **Prayer focus:** Those who are tempted to compare themselves and their situation to others.

4

Gaining a Cents of Worth

Occasionally I'll get a touch of gas. When I'm in the company of others this can be embarrassing. For them, I mean.

Recently my buddy Pat and I were anchored in Oriental harbor, each of us working on a best-selling novel, when Pat decided to stretch his legs.

You can only walk around the deck of my thirty-foot sailboat so many times before you become bored, so he suggested we dinghy into town. The characters in my book were asleep or dead anyway — it's hard to tell the way my plot plods along — so I agreed to go with him. We hitched the small outboard to the stern of my inflatable and motored over to the fuel pumps at Oriental Marina. I left Pat with the dinghy and then walked across the lawn towards the marina office.

You know how sometimes when you walk alone, you think no one is watching or no one's close enough to hear? Well, I thought I was by myself as I walked up the patio steps towards the building. At least I hoped I was alone. What I was doing was shameful. Pat thought so, too. That's why he'd stayed in the dinghy.

But it turned out I wasn't alone. Joe Wright heard me coming. He thought I was just another gas customer, but I'm never just another anything. I'm my own "special Ed" case. Joe hid behind the bar as I walked by.

When I explained to the guy in the office what I wanted, he told me to hurry back outside and look for Joe. I think he wanted me out of his office. I think he thought I was bad for business. I found Joe and he stood there listening to me, taking it like the man his wife wishes he was.

"I need some gas," I explained.

"In your sailboat?" he asked.

"No, in my dinghy."

We stopped at the pumps where I'd parked the dinghy. Pat was on the seat cowering in embarrassment.

"Where's your auxiliary tank?" Joe asked.

"My cousin Milton has it. He took it off the boat when he thought we were going to get hit with another hurricane, and he never brought it back. He has one of my surfboards too."

"So you just want to fill that small tank on top of the outboard?"

"Yes. There's still some in it but not much. I'd hate to run out. Be kind of embarrassing."

Joe looked over at me and then towards Pat, and rolled his eyes. Then he uncoiled the gas hose and handed me the nozzle. It took ten seconds to fill 'er up.

"Whoa wee, Eddie. You got two tenths of a gallon," Joe said with mock astonishment.

"Really? Is that all? I swear it looked almost empty."

"Probably was. That tank holds, what, a quarter of a gallon?"

I gave Joe a five-dollar bill and told him to keep the change, but he returned from the office in a few minutes.

"I can't keep the rest of your money, Eddie. Obviously you need it more than me. That small amount of gas only cost you thirty-nine cents, but it probably cost my boss ten times that in labor. I'd have to say you're about the cheapest (and then Joe used a word I can't repeat) I've ever met."

Joe's right. I am cheap. When I accepted Christ I became heir with him in his father's kingdom, but you couldn't prove it by the way I live. I spend most of what I earn on myself, complain that those who are poor should get a job, and wish the illiterate would get an education. I freely give my opinion to all who'll listen, but I seldom offer a word of encouragement to those who are hurting. I wish I was a better example of Christ. I wish I lived as if I believed I was the son of God. But I'm afraid Joe nailed me for what I am.

A penny-pinching sailor.

Most marina operators dislike sailboaters because we pull into their marina with laundry hanging from the lifelines, unload garbage into their trash bins and then let our dog poop on their grass. We top off our water tanks after buying five dollars' worth of diesel, and then complain that the price of diesel is too high. If sailors have a reputation for being cheap, then I'm their poster child. My Topsiders have holes in the soles, I putter around in a hand-me-down dinghy, and for several years I stayed in a free slip at Whittaker Creek. It drew only two feet of water and was constantly under siege by mosquitoes, but Cutter's was cheaper than slip rent. I'm in a nicer slip now, using docklines that were left by the previous renter. Last week I saw a Taylor boat fender floating in the river, so I picked it up. Now I have four boat fenders, none of which match, but they're all in excellent condition.

After I got gas that afternoon we walked up the street to M & M's. Zarah came to wait on our table, and when she saw it was me, she asked if I wanted the usual.

"What's the usual?" I asked, testing her.

"Corn crab chowder soup, lots of rolls, and water with a lemon."

I nodded. She rolled her eyes — rolled them the way Joe did that afternoon. Rolled them the way my friend did when he gave me the dinghy and four-stroke outboard. Rolled them the way Pat does every time he rides with me to town. The way we look in public can say a lot about a person.

From the reaction I'm getting these days, it looks like I'm cheap.

➤ **Hard Aground hint:** We are born naked, hungry, and poor. Buy a boat and chances are, you'll stay that way.

➤ **Passage markers:** *If you want to be perfect, go, sell your possessions and give to the poor, and you will have treasure in heaven. Then come, follow me.* —Matthew 19:21. For further inspiration read Mark 12:41–44.

➤ **Prayer focus:** Those who are poor in possessions but rich in service to others.

5

Eternal Shoalmates

YOU WOULDN'T THINK SOMETHING LIKE A SIMPLE SANDBAR GROUNDING could entertain a village for more than a century or two, but then you'd have to know a little something about the people of our settlement and the North Carolina coast to understand.

It all started as I was dragging a deck chair onto the grass beside the Dockhouse. We call the patch of brown lawn beside the dockmaster's office the lounge area because there's a rotten bench and a few plastic chairs and a flagpole with a frayed halyard. Nobody ever eats there except the mosquitoes and sand fleas, and only then when some fool tourist stops to take a picture of the sun melting into the mounds of mud flats across the creek on Carrot Island. Mostly it's just a place to share a cold drink with a few friends and watch the boat traffic work its way up and down the channel.

Traffic's been heavy recently, with everyone scrambling to get pieces of eight, a piece of the Queen's plate, or at the very least, a piece of immortality. From deep-sea divers to head-boat captains, folks in Beaufort and Morehead City have been angling their way over to that sliver of shoal cradling the most famous shipwreck on the Carolina coast. It's a waste of time, if you ask me, since nothing's safe on these barrier islands except endangered wildlife and the regulations that protect them. The way I figure it, any gold hidden in the bowels of the *Queen Anne's Revenge* was whisked away long ago by the currents that scour the Outer Banks.

19

Still, the startling news of the pirate shipwreck was the break I needed to combat this charge that my navigational impotence was a disgrace to the armada of busybodies sailing along the Carolina coast. Henceforth and forevermore, nautical neophytes like myself can run aground as far and as often as we like, and never again feel guilty for our stupidity and carelessness. Now we have a free pass — a gift from the eternal host of all sandbar parties. From now on, my little indiscretions will pale in comparison to the granddaddy of all astounding groundings. I'm speaking, of course, of that terror of the high seas, Blackbeard himself, who beached it but good off Beaufort Inlet and sank his boat in the process. Poor guy. It couldn't have happened to a more cunning cutthroat.

My first thought on hearing the news that it was Beaufort Inlet where Blackbeard sank his boat so long ago was to conjure up a vision of the Great One tumbling out of his bunk, his wiry beard soiled with stale saliva.

"What in Grandma Drummond's dram shot have you run into this time, Hawkins?" he'd probably asked, his eyes still blistered from a brutal bout with some cheap rum.

"From the slope of the deck and the pitch of the mast, sir, it appears to be an island of some sort that has lost its struggle to stay afloat."

"Are you saying we have run aground on a shoal?"

"It would appear so, Captain."

"Were we anticipating any shoals in this channel, sailor?"

"Well, sir, we're not exactly in the channel."

"Not in the channel?"

"No sir. The channel is over there between those green and red markers."

"Well, why in Haiti's hilltops didn't you take this vessel down the channel, sailor?"

"Because when we departed New Providence you ordered the crew to hold this heading until you sobered up. Sorry, sir, we didn't think it would take you this long."

"Well, never mind all that. My new orders are for you to follow the channel through the pass, paying careful attention to clear this shoal that's fixed itself to our keel. If word of this grounding gets out I'll be the laughingstock of every pub from here to Havana."

"Aye, aye, Captain. Got to protect your dignity and honor and all."

"Exactly."

Well, who knows for certain what happened the night Blackbeard ran aground off Beaufort, North Carolina, but it would have been his style to spread the blame around. Any skipper worth a cuss would do the same. It's a known fact that Blackbeard made a lucrative living relieving Spanish galleons of their cargo as they sailed up the Carolina coast. Blackbeard worked the shoals and shipping lanes the way former UNC basketball coach Dean Smith used to work a TV timeout. He was crafty and cold-blooded and as ruthless a scoundrel as you'd ever want to meet — I'm speaking of Blackbeard, you understand.

So you can understand my delight when I learned that the Great One himself, my mentor and master, was prone to taking sandbar soundings with the keel of his vessel. The sad fact is my reputation as a skilled navigator has suffered considerably from my litany of "Hard Aground" confessions. But at last I have a clever rebuttal to all those nasty comments I receive when I come up short of water.

"Oh yeah? You think I planted her good?" I'll shout back the next time I've uncovered a sunken shoal. "Well I'm not as bad as Blackbeard. I never lost a boat. At least not for more than a day or two, and even if I did, the thing was still floating when I found it again. So back off, Bub."

I wish I'd have known about the sinking of *Queen Anne's Revenge* on my first passage home from the Bahamas. We had enjoyed a pleasant sail north from the Abacos, catching a nice lift when we hit the Gulf Stream. A little after midnight, lured by the glittering lights of the beach homes on Atlantic Beach, I drew close to shore in search of our first set of markers. The captain was asleep, but when he sensed the change in swell direction he came on deck to verify our position.

"What's your heading?"

"Don't really have one," I said. "I'm just running parallel to the coast until we reach the markers off our bow. Then we can fall off and head down the channel."

He peered into the darkness beyond the bow, and then went below to secure our latest coordinates. I saw him note the longitude on the legal pad and plot our position on the paper chart. Then he rubbed the stubble on his chin and looked out to sea.

"Do me a favor," he asked. "Turn ninety degrees and let's head due south."

"Why?"

"Because we're about to run aground."

"What?"

"The entrance to the inlet is out there. See?"

Sure enough, befuddled by darkness, fatigue, and a false sense of security, I finally saw the dim glimmer of red and green sea buoys off to my right.

"Why didn't you stay on the heading I gave you earlier?" he asked.

"I thought we were almost home."

"Well, you thought wrong."

Staying the course and finishing strong is a rare quality in our culture. Athletes dance and strut — and sometimes lose games by celebrating too early. The less notable middle-class man stashes away six percent of his income in a 401K account and then retires, only to find himself a few years later working the checkout lane at Home Depot because the race to the end got longer.

It's a hard thing to keep at a task that seems to have no end, and yet the Apostle Paul called us to run the good race. To finish strong. To serve to the end, making no provision for the future except for the hope we have in Christ. It's a tough business to continue on in darkness and not be led astray by the sparkle and lure of lights, but that's the course marked before us. God is the magnetic north on our compass and the Holy Spirit is the needle pointing us to him. Our job is to adjust our course to align with the needle and when we do this, we'll always find our way home.

I thought I was home that night. I thought I knew better than the captain. I thought wrong.

I would have sure looked stupid running aground near Beaufort after such a smooth sail home, but I'd look even dumber if I came up short of the goals God has placed before me.

When it comes to sorry sailors, though, at least I'm not the only fool to miss the Beaufort Channel. The top honors, it turns out, belong to Blackbeard.

So the next time I come back from the islands I'll probably have another go at that sandbar, and if I get stuck, it'll be comforting to know that I'm wallowing in the wake of an eternal shoalmate.

I just hope I don't have to wallow too long.

For more information on the preservation and recovery of *Queen Anne's Revenge* visit the North Carolina Department of Cultural Resources website at www.ah.dcr.state.nc.us/qar/

➤ **Hard Aground hint:** The trip is never over until the anchor is set.

➤ **Passage markers:** *Do you not know that in a race all the runners run, but only one gets the prize? Run in such a way as to get the prize.* —1 Corinthians 9:24. For further inspiration read: Hebrews 12:1–3.

➤ **Prayer focus:** Those tempted to quit on God before he's brought them into port.

6

(Sand)Bar Hopping

I DON'T KNOW WHAT THE LADY IN THE PINK BLOUSE EXPECTED TO SEE that Saturday morning as she rested her elbows atop the starboard railing of the Cedar Island ferry.

Oh, she might have hoped to catch sight of a school of dolphins playing in the prop wash as she tossed breadcrumbs to hungry seagulls. A lot of passengers go for that sort of thing. Or she could've hoped to spend a few minutes alone with an early morning sunrise. A lot of folks like that too. For all I know she might have needed to pitch her grits over the side of the ferry in an unladylike manner. I've seen a few tourists do that as well. Who can say for certain what she expected to see?

Maybe she wanted one last look at the purple shoreline of Ocracoke as the sun rose over the Atlantic, or maybe she wasn't looking at anything at all. Maybe she was just resting there with her brain in neutral as she gazed across Pamlico Sound. There's no saying for certain what she expected to see as she leaned into the coolness of the morning. But what caught her attention was of such wonder and amazement that it sent her into a frenzy of excitement, compelling her to sprint through the maze of parked vehicles to her own blue Ford pickup, where she yanked open the back of the Leonard camper shell to extract three small children.

As if suddenly ignited by a sugar fix, the youngsters bolted from the truck, almost crushing an old man resting against the hood of his car. Because

24

a crowd had begun to gather along the boat's railing, the children clambered up and onto the roof of the camper. When the smallest child could stand it no longer, he broke rank and lifted a timid hand to wave.

I was leaning over the bow of my sailboat and tugging at the anchor line when I looked up and saw his shy gesture of recognition. I ceased my labor, straightened up, and waved back at the boy with all the dignity I could muster. I took a moment to wipe the sweat from my face, and then I watched as the ferry passed, wondering how I would rate in that small boy's summer vacation adventures. I hoped I would rate high.

"Grandma," the boy might begin as he recounted his trip, "you should have been with us on vacation last week. We drove to the Outer Banks and got to see these sand dunes big as mountains where they killed devils one time. And real close by was a place where they flew the first airplane. Next we stayed in a campground that had this huge lighthouse that used to sit right on the beach. Mom says they moved it so it wouldn't fall down, but I don't see how they could. It's too big. Dad tried to teach us to fish, but we didn't catch anything except some new fishing words Dad used when he baited his thumb. When we finally got tired of catching no fish we drove down to where Blackbeard the Pirate used to live. He's not there anymore, but I don't think the people on the island know it because there are stores that still have lots of his stuff. I think they're waiting for him to come back.

"Best of all, Grandma, on the day we left to come home on the big ferryboat, I saw a man in a sailboat camping on this tiny island. I asked mom if I could go camping on an island like that, except in a tent. She said the man wasn't supposed to be there. That he must've gotten confused and ran aground. Maybe he did, Grandma, but it sure looked fun."

Sure, it's easy to laugh about it now. I only wish the crowd on the ferry had held their laughter that day. Cheering crowds can restore the spirit of a defeated team, and I've learned that to be an encouragement to others, sometimes you have to live through life's Astounding Groundings. The beauty of a sunset is reflected on the underbelly of clouds — the splendor of a rainbow filtered through the prism of a storm.

Over the years I've become something of an expert on the ways a person can become navigationally stuck, and I've noticed there is a scoring system in place to gauge how well someone accomplishes this task. In fact, you've probably used it once or twice yourself and didn't even know it. It's called the Hard Aground Heart Ache — Ha-Ha! — and here is how it works.

It's a sunny day with little wind, no rain, and all the promise of a great cruise. You've got a chart down below with precise compass headings clearly marked from previous trips, but you've made this run so often that navigating this stretch of water is like driving home from work. You can do it with your eyes closed. So you do. You engage the autopilot, grab a book, and build a nest up under the dodger. You dab some sunscreen on the tops of your feet and begin that novel you've been meaning to read, getting past the introduction and most of the first chapter before it hits you — or rather, you hit it.

The boat lurches forward in that sickening manner that lets you know that you've run out of water. You jump up and look around only to discover that you're a good twenty feet on the wrong side of the marker. Well, you do what you always do in these situations — you cuss. Then you slam her into reverse and begin trying to extract yourself from this stupid blunder.

On the Ha Ha scale this maneuver will fetch you only the minimum score. You see, it's based on carelessness and complacency and requires little imagination. Any fool can perform this stunt, and many do with great frequency. Tell this story over a round of drinks at the next yacht club meeting, and it might start a few heads nodding and get you a chuckle or two, but that's all. It's your basic half pike in the Astounding Grounding category.

When we pass someone featured along the edge of a channel in this manner, we seldom give them a second look. It's obvious the boat's stuck, and equally obvious the crew will get it floating again. The crew is in no danger, they're just inconvenienced, so it's a stupid stuck and of no concern to anyone.

Getting sucked out of the channel on a falling tide by a three-knot current gets you a better score. You'll see this one performed a lot around inlets. We all ache a little when we see a vessel listing to one side under full sail, and realize she's not moving. It gets our attention and tugs at our heart. Unlike the stupid stuck, this one is worth a second look, and warrants a five on the Ha-Ha scale. If the boat was under sail when the skipper saw he was having trouble, however, and he refused to start the engine because he thinks motoring is for weenies, then deduct two points for pride and arrogance. Our sport requires prudence and sound judgment, and without some rules and regulations stupid skippers would begin staging stunts like this just to gain a higher score. If, on the other hand, the engine died while he was making his way through the inlet, and the crew tried to sail in, then add one point for creativity and perseverance.

Running aground while reading a chart is a tough one to score. All the information is there on the chart, but the contestant gets stuck anyway. While other athletic events might view this as sloppy technique, we do not, since reading a chart is one of boating's more difficult tasks. Still, we are supposed to know this stuff, so running aground because you can't read the chart gets you nothing but a sympathetic nod, or maybe a free drink. Competitors in this event often appear "dumb stuck" upon discovery, as if they haven't a clue as to how they got there — which, of course, they don't. Participants in this event are not highly regarded within the sailing community. They also make up a majority of boaters. Score this one a three.

Night groundings automatically get you a five, since everything is magnified at night except the channel markers. Contestants in night navigation demonstrate both confidence and a quest for adventure. The real potential in night groundings is in seeing how far you can launch a boat out of the channel before running aground. Sometimes distances of thirty to forty yards can be attained before you land. This type of maneuver is guaranteed to turn heads and get the crowd talking. Add a point for comments like, "Do you think he meant to be in this hemisphere?" Add another point for driving around in the dark while trying to get back to the channel before finally planting the bow in a spot worse than before. You can't fully appreciate the difficulty of this technique until daybreak and low tide reveal you are at the headwaters of a small creek in the Appalachians. Add two more points for this nifty maneuver.

Any grounding showing bare hull down to the keel gets a point, no questions asked.

Well now you're stuck, but that's only half the game. Getting unstuck offers the competitor an opportunity to increase his score. Kedging off with a dinghy and anchor demonstrates self-reliance and prudence and is rewarded with high marks. Looking pathetic and begging for help from the bow of your boat will only expose you for the weenie you are. Ours is a demanding sport and not intended for the faint of heart. Gaining the assistance of a power boater is allowed, but only if you maintain a sense of dignity during the ordeal. Loudly screaming "By golly, my next boat is going to be a Grady-White" will only expose you for the amateur that you are and gain you little with the critics. Remember, you are being graded on the manner and theme of your exhibition as well as your technique. A bonus of three points is given to anyone liberated by the U.S. Coast Guard, since this prestigious government agency no longer officially takes responsibility for extracting ignorant mariners from clearly marked shoals.

Now that we have established how the game is scored, let's see how I fared that day. I'll take five points for a night grounding, two more for driving around and planting the keel further from the channel, and another three for being hauled off by the Coast Guard. Subtract two for trying to sail down the channel with a fully functional engine, but add a point back for attempting to read the chart and not understanding it. Finally, give me a point for exposing the full length of my keel for all to see. That makes 10. A perfect score!

Thank goodness God doesn't judge us by our mistakes. He looks at our heart. In the book of James the author warns, "Suppose a man comes into your meeting wearing a gold ring and fine clothes, and a poor man in shabby clothes also comes in. If you show special attention to the man wearing fine clothes and say, 'Here's a good seat for you,' but say to the poor man, 'You stand there' or 'Sit on the floor by my feet,' have you not discriminated among yourselves and become judges with evil thoughts? . . . Has not God chosen those who are poor in the eyes of the world to be rich in faith and to inherit the kingdom he promised those who love him?"

The key is to go forth, try and fail, and then sail on. Mistakes will be made, but God can perfect a man who puts his whole trust in him, goes forth, and perseveres. That, in summary, is the life of every great man and woman of faith. That can be your life, too.

➤ **Hard Aground hint:** Our mistakes can serve as a warning to others, though this is not a field of ministry I would recommend.

➤ **Passage markers:** *But the Lord said to Samuel, "Do not consider his appearance or his height. . . . The Lord does not look at the things man looks at. Man looks on the outward appearance, but the Lord looks on the heart.* —1 Samuel 16:7. For further inspiration read 1 Samuel 16:1–13.

➤ **Prayer focus:** Those who feel their motives are misunderstood and their mistakes amplified.

7

Anchors Away

I CAN'T STOP CRUISING.

Believe me, I've tried, but every time I drop my anchor the boat accelerates through the harbor, out the channel, and off to another port, leaving me to wonder why this oversized fishhook hanging off the bow can't seem to get a grip, or at least a clue, as to its function and purpose. It's a good thing I'm hooked on boating, because I'm never hooked on anything at the bottom.

The late Dick Bradley of *Motor Boating and Sailing* once said, "If God had meant for man to anchor he would have made all harbors a uniform twelve feet deep with firm, sandy bottoms, no adverse currents or sudden wind shifts, no hidden underwater snares such as cables, pieces of chain, old anchors, rocks, tree stumps or grassy patches.

"But, as any of you who have anchored can testify," Bradley concluded, "there's no doubt in anyone's mind exactly where God stands on this particular subject."

It's obvious Dick was a religious man, or at least a Methodist, and knew a little something about anchoring. Since I can't stop my boat the old-fashioned way, I've perfected what I call the Fred Flintstone Braking System. This technique requires shallow water, flat feet, and soft mud. It begins when I sail through a tranquil fleet, dodging sterns and stares in search of a narrow slot in which to park my small sloop. With the headsail bulging, mainsheet cranked in tight, and helm lashed with a bungee cord, I completely terrorize the neighborhood and then rush to the bow to release my small anchor. This is mostly for show since, as I've explained already, the hook almost never catches. Next I casually stroll back to the cockpit, unshackle the helm, and point the bow towards the nearest shoal. When the keel is firmly planted in the mud and my boat shutters to a stop, I settle down on a seat cushion and take a nap.

When I encounter a bottom coated in oysters or coral, I have to modify this approach, since it takes a few minutes to tackle my wife, loop a line around her waist, and toss her into the water. Once her bare feet have dislodged the first layer of oysters, she stays put, and given her size and weight, she quickly overpowers the flagging momentum of our boat. If tug-of-war were an Olympic sport, Bennie's face would be on a box of Wheaties.

When Bennie and I first began cruising we tried to anchor like everyone else. That is to say, we shouted at each other and cussed a lot. I remember one afternoon attempting to anchor on the back side of Christmas Tree Island in Key West. We were trying to nudge up close to the shore so we could enjoy the festive sounds echoing down Duval Street and, as was my habit in those days, I was on the bow directing the disaster.

It was my job to look for a firm, sandy spot and holler at Bennie so she would know when it was time to back down. (Sometimes she tells me to back down, but this is usually later in the evening.) Anyway, I was calling the signals and she was shaking them off when suddenly I realized that our boat was caught in a crosscurrent that was carrying us around the point. I yanked the pin that held the anchor in place and watched the chain and rope slide through the bow roller until the last of the line leapt over the side and disappeared. Someone had forgotten to attach the rope to the eyebolt in the anchor well.

Because I was too stupid to know better, I dove in, yelling and clawing my way to the bottom until I found the line lying on the sand. By the time I finished toweling off and changing into dry shorts, Bennie had the anchor line snubbed down and all the scattered rope secured. Of course, by then the sunset over the Marquesas Islands had clouded over, and it was starting to rain on my dry outfit, so I headed back to the V-berth where I found my bride peeling off her swimsuit. I offered to help, but was told it was my turn to back down, so I retreated to the cockpit and sat in the rain.

Some months later I was returning from Cape Lookout when the boys and I encountered a severe line of thunderducks paddling across our bow. Now according to the U.S. Power Squadron book of seamanship, the proper procedure when threatened by a fleet of dawdling ducks is to sign them up as squadron members, but I ignored this advice and shortened sail anyway. We were almost at the end of our cruise, so I decided to empty the galley of all remaining food items in the hopes that the commune of cockroaches living in our boat would leave. It's a scientific fact that the average cockroach has the same chemical dependency on snack food as a teenage boy and will eat anything, including a small child, that is left unwrapped. Packaging doesn't deter teenage boys, and that is the principal difference between a boy and a cockroach.

Well anyway, I spent too long cleaning out the cupboards because when I finally went topside our sailboat was about to hit land. I ordered my eldest son to take the helm while I ran forward to deploy the anchor. The flukes caught immediately, which surprised us all, so I backwinded the main and went forward to cleat off the anchor line. That's when the tail end of the rope popped up from its hole, slithered across my foot, and darted through the bow chock and over the side of our boat. Someone had, again, forgotten to attach it to the eyebolt in the anchor well.

I'm aware that the proper term for the tail end of a rope is the "bitter end" and, having neglected to secure that part of the rope numerous times now, I've come to appreciate the origin of the phrase. But anchors aren't the only things I've tossed aside.

I've tossed away a perfectly good compliment when my boys were in need of encouragement. I've thrown away an opportunity to teach a Bible study because it conflicted with my cruising schedule. I've failed to secure my opinion when a friend was looking for comfort and hope rather than criticism and honesty. And I've selfishly hoarded the talents and gifts God has given me, using them on myself rather than on the people God has placed in my life.

Jesus said that to whom much is given much will be expected. That he who has much will receive more, but that he who does not have, even what little he has will be taken away. God is a shrewd manager. He holds us accountable for our time and talents, and too often we spend these on ourselves. God did not create me to serve myself. He created me to serve others. We are all called to be the hands and feet of God — to see others through his eyes and serve him by serving others. To toss away an opportunity to serve others is to miss out on the best part of life.

Tossing away a perfectly good anchor remains my most public display of stupidity (although apparently I'm not the only one who does this sort of thing). Last winter I was down in the British Virgin Islands sitting through another hot skipper's meeting when my charter instructor made a special point to demonstrate the proper way to retrieve an anchor with a windlass. I've never owned a boat large enough to need a windlass, so I was paying particular attention to make certain I came home with all my fingers intact in case Bennie ever wanted help getting out of her swimsuit. My instructor was explaining how we were responsible for all the equipment assigned to the boat and he made a special point to emphasize how expensive the anchors were, as though I was going to try to smuggle one home on the plane. When I made a joke about trying to boost his quiver of CQRs, he stopped the presentation, looked up from the chart, and pointed his finger at me.

"Dis isn't funny, mon. You be surprised how many anchors we lose in a week."

"The bottom at Norman Island isn't that fluky, is it?" I asked.

"No, but you charter people are. At least once a week we get a customer calling to ask if we will bring over a few more anchors. I had a guy call dis morning begging us to bring over de rest of his allotment. I asked what he'd done with de ones dat were on de boat and he said he'd left 'em on de bottom at Peter Island. He tought dat's what he was supposed to do, dat he was supposed to leave dem behind for de next guy. He tought de moorings grew up from discarded anchors. Can you imagine someone dat stupid actually owning a boat?"

No, I can't. And I hope you won't either.

➤ **Hard Aground hint:** "God protects children and fools and loves both equally. He must or he wouldn't have made so many of us." —ANONYMOUS

➤ **Passage markers:** *His master replied, "Well done, good and faithful servant!*

You have been faithful with a few things; I will put you in charge of many things. Come and share your master's happiness. —Matthew 25:21. For further inspiration read the rest of the passage, Matthew 25:14–30.

➤ **Prayer focus:** Those tempted to throw away the gifts, talents, and time God has given them.

What I want in a chart is lots of pretty blue grids overlaid with phrases like "Deep protected anchorage here, approach from any direction" and "Firm bottom with good water up to the shoreline." I don't see much of this on the charts I have. The cruising guides I own are littered with ominous warnings along the lines of "Extensive shoals, restricted area, submerged wreck" and "Military bombing range." Descriptions like these discourage me from sailing in such areas.

Part II

Signal Flags: "Tiller" Communications

8

Hand-Held Navigational Aids

SOMETIME LATER THIS WINTER, I'M GOING TO TAKE A FEW DAYS OFF TO study the cruising guides of all the places I've sailed to this year. There's no point reading about a place I haven't visited yet, since the range markers and channel depths don't mean anything to me. I have to know enough about a place to be confused before reading the directions helps. Once I've mistaken the float of a crab trap for a channel marker or tied up in Bubba Grump's shrimp-boat slip, then I can make some sense of the warnings offered in the cruising manuals. It will be fun now to see if the experts had any good advice.

Some people think reading a chart is the first thing you should do when planning a passage, but I think this is a bad idea. All the chart is going to tell you is where others have been, or where you can't go, and I already have a wife who does that for me. Or if I'm confused and in doubt as to my destination, Bennie is perfectly willing to tell me where to go. I don't think even the most expensive electronic chart could replace her clear and candid comments.

What I want in a chart is lots of pretty blue grids overlaid with phrases like "Deep protected anchorage here, approach from any direction" and "Firm bottom with good water up to the shoreline." I don't see much of this on the charts I have. The cruising guides I own are littered with ominous warnings along the lines of "Extensive shoals, restricted area, submerged wreck" and "Military bombing range." Descriptions like these discourage me from sailing in such areas. Often I'm tempted to leave these charts and guides aboard

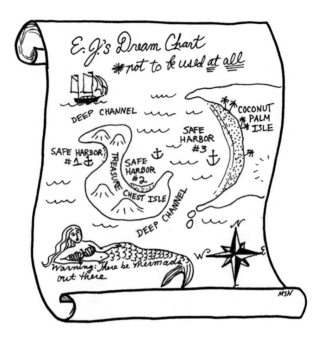

when I sell the boat, but the next crew could become disheartened, so I take them with me. If Columbus had believed half of what was scribbled on his flat maps, Americans would be socialist and French and demanding a twenty-hour workweek.

People who read charts and follow the advice in the cruising guides are usually the same crowd who eat frozen yogurt instead of ice cream. They have the boatyard change the oil in their diesel and, while they might live longer and have a drawer of clean tee shirts, they'll never lose a lounge chair to a shoal that suddenly rises from the sea. To find the secret riches of Atlantis you have to sail beyond the edge of the chart, and in my brief career as a coastal explorer, I have uncovered a number of treasure islands just below the water's surface.

Cruising by its very nature should be an intuitive process, something as natural as drooling on a pillow or passing gas in your sleep, but I've found that coastal navigation requires a little more effort than that. So here are a few suggestions to help reduce the stress of skinny-water sailing.

First, we should abandon the red and green marking method. It's an antiquated system that was probably imported by the French and is utterly confusing to everyone except the frozen yogurt crowd who learned this stuff in a U.S. Power Squadron boating course. I know a little about "red right returning," but I've noticed this rule can vary depending on whether you're coming or going from a channel, continent, or a creekside bar. The sheer volume of exceptions to this "red right" rule exceeds even the excessive number of grammatical guidelines governing the simple spelling of a word like "there/their/they're."

A few years ago I was chauffeuring my crew back to our sailboat in a dinghy via a channel that leads to the sea. Our anchorage was the main attraction along this route, since the inlet was almost shoaled shut and barely a viable cut to the ocean. The Army Corps of Engineers didn't see it that way, though. If you were to believe their channel markings I was about to embark on an around-the-world cruise in a leaky inflatable with a crew of tipsy merry-maids who needed to relieve themselves. Every time I angled the dinghy over to the wrong side of a red marker, which was the right side in my view, I would run aground on a shoal, spilling the girls onto the sand. This detour offered the ladies the opportunity to stretch their legs, but I think better traffic signs — and less beer — would have been of more use. As an alternative to the red/green-nun/can-do Christmas tree decorating design, I recommend we use simple hand signs.

A wooden hand cutout of about two feet in diameter, with the index finger pointing towards deep water, would show the way to the main channel. Two hands on the same pole with fingers pointing in either direction would indicate that both sides of the piling had good depth. Such a sign would also designate a fork in the channel, so distances to competing destinations and a billboard or two would be welcomed at such intersections. A palm-up hand sign, like the gesture given by a school crossing guard, would warn of an area with shallow water. A thumbs-down placard would identify a harbor with restricted anchoring patrolled by snooty condo dwellers. I'm sure you can think of other hand signs that might work just as well. With simple hand-holding like this, even the navigationally challenged could find their way back to deep water.

When I'm spiritually stuck, I prefer flashing lights to dull signposts, clear choices to vague hunches, and confirming circumstances to hazy happenings.

I seldom get this kind of clear guidance, though. What I get instead is the word of God, some gentle nudging from the Holy Spirit, and sound counsel from Christian friends. What's surprising is that this is usually enough to get me moving back into deep water.

God doesn't promise that we'll escape the shoals of life — only that when we become stuck, he'll come alongside to pull us off. The temptation, for me, is to take the shortcut and skip the hard lessons that come with the long passage of testing. To think that when Christ said, "I come that they may have life, and have it abundantly," that somehow means that all my days will be sunny and storm-free.

When he was led into the desert for his forty days of testing, Christ too was tempted to take the shortcut. He was tempted to take control of his situation by making bread from stones, to demand that God preserve him by taking a foolish leap of faith, and to seek power and prestige in something other than the will of his father. Jesus resisted on all counts — thank God he did. In taking the long, hard route he became for me and for all of us a savior and the ultimate towing package. He's been there, done that and knows the depths of our despair. When it comes to finding a friend who'll stick by you when you're stuck in a bad way, Christ is the best kind of shoalmate.

➤ **Hard Aground hint:** Never use your keel to test the water's depth on a falling tide.

➤ **Passage markers:** *Trust in the Lord with all your heart, and lean not on your own understanding; in all your ways acknowledge Him, and He will make your paths straight.* —Proverbs 3:5–6. For further inspiration read Psalms 32:7–11.

➤ **Prayer focus:** Those seeking God's clear direction for some decision in their lives.

9

I Don't Know, Bub, Sounds Fishy to Me

NORTH CAROLINA HAS AN ACUTE FISH SHORTAGE. FISH, AS YOU KNOW, are small sea-habitat creatures that assemble in schools and struggle to answer such basic questions as:

What is the purpose of a belt loop? If you want to work in the fast-food industry what foreign language should you take? What was rock 'n' roll music and how did the Monkees kill it?

No, wait. Those are the stupid groupers slouching in the halls of my son's school. What I meant to say is that saltwater fish are an endangered species that need our protection. We know this because people, mostly men, keep trying to catch fish and can't. That's why the state of North Carolina studied the saltwater fishing problem extensively — or at least almost a whole day — and determined that a special government assistance program was needed to help fishermen catch more fish.

You may recall from your study of U.S. history that fishing was the core principle upon which this country was founded. Christopher Columbus was actually serving as independent counsel for King Ferdinand when he embarked on a fishing expedition and strayed from his original mission. He discovered North America instead of fish, so he claimed India for Spain and that's why you should take Spanish if you want to work at Burger King. It's also why Native Americans are called Indians and why Whitewater is no longer just a rafting term.

But never mind that. What we're discussing today is our state's saltwater fishing crisis and how we're going to fix it. North Carolina has taken the bold step of following the lead of other states and passed a law requiring saltwater fishermen to carry a license when drowning shrimp. This new fish license will raise millions of dollars, none of which will be used to teach fish how to get caught, because that would make way too much sense. Instead most of the money will be used to catch people fishing without a license. A small portion of the money will also be used to sponsor next year's Saltwater Fish-a-Thon.

What is the Saltwater Fish-a-Thon? It's a new program sponsored by the Division of Marine Fisheries that employs a team of out-of-work IT processionals to randomly call people during the dinner hour. This new program should vastly improve the frequency and intensity of dinner interruptions, making this year's Saltwater Fish-a-Thon the biggest and best ever. I imagine a call might go something like this.

"Excuse me, but I see that you recently purchased a saltwater fishing license at the Neuse Sports Shop. Would you mind telling me how many fish you caught on that trip to the coast last Labor Day?"

"Uh-huh."

"Ah . . . uh-huh what?"

"Uh-huh, I mind telling you."

"Why's that?"

"Can't say."

"You mean you can't say why you mind telling me if you caught any fish last year?"

"Right."

"How come?"

"It's complicated."

"You didn't catch as many as you told your brother-in-law, did you?"

"Something like that."

"And they weren't really that big, were they?"

"Not exactly."

"So you lied about your catch."

"I'm not saying one way or the other. And don't call me again."

"Oh, but I will. You're in our database, Bub."

With harassment of this sort you can see why some are calling for an alternative to the saltwater fishing license. I think I've found just the solution.

Light.

Light is cheap and abundant and anyone can use it with a little training. Best of all, you don't need a license to use light.

I discovered this wonderful product last month when my buddy Pat and I were sailing his boat out of Oriental harbor. We'd parked his twenty-foot day sailor at the dinghy dock and walked up the street to M & M's for dinner. A few hours later as we pulled away from the dock I flashed the light across the water towards the main channel. Suddenly fish began to jump up and down the way a forty-year-old woman might at a Clay Aiken concert.

"Hey Pat, look at those jumping fish," I said, hoping he wouldn't notice that I'd wrapped the battery cable around the centerboard drum.

"They're attracted to the light. Would you please shine it on that marker so I don't run into the jetty?"

"Yeah, sure. But isn't this cool?"

"Getting this boat back to the marina would be cooler."

Just then a fish dove into our boat. No kidding, a fish just jumped out of the water and landed in the bottom of the boat.

"Throw it back," he said, untangling the battery cable. "And shine the light on this mess you've made. I can't drop the centerboard with that wire wrapped around the drum, and we're about to run into the rocks."

I was still holding the light on the water when two more fish jumped in. Now I don't know much about fishing, but I thought it was pretty strange that fish would jump into our boat even though I didn't have a license. Maybe fish don't know about the new law, or don't really care.

Sometimes I'll land a blessing this way too. I'll be working on a problem, trying to hook a solution that is just beyond the reach of my skills, when suddenly a blessing will jump in my boat. I've received free automobiles, a dinghy, an outboard motor, several sailboats, a wife, furniture, and good health.

Landing a blessing is a little like hooking a fish. We have to launch our boat and sail away from shore, moving out into the deep waters where the risk is greater. Great blessings are seldom found in shallow pools. If you're fishing for lobster you have to dive into the dark crevasses. That's where you'll find adventure for a lifetime and food for a day. Jesus calls us into the boat and away from land. He calls us to move beyond our comfort zone, to cast our net in the deep waters and to trust him to fill our needs. It's a daily prayer that he answers with large fish some days and lots of little fish other times.

But it's almost a certainty that we won't catch the big fish or big blessings standing on the beach. We have to move out, take a risk, and trust that he'll provide for our needs. Mission work is a risk. Marriage is a risk. Tithing is a risk. Sharing the Gospel is a risk. Yet God has promised to bless us when we venture forth, open our hearts, and cast our nets into the water.

In the sixth chapter of the Gospel of Mark there is fishing story. More than five thousand people have gathered for an outdoor revival, and the disciples come to Jesus to suggest that he send the people away so they can buy dinner for themselves. But Jesus answers, "You give them something to eat." The disciples are stunned. They don't have the money or time to provide for so many, and ATM machines haven't been invented yet.

So Jesus takes the two fish and five hamburger buns from a small boy and feeds the five thousand. This is often where the story and sermons stop. But following that covered-dish supper, Jesus does a surprising thing. He immediately tells his fishermen-disciples to get in a fishing boat and row across a fishing lake to a town called — and this is where I grin — Bethsaida, which in Hebrew means, fish town. And you know what? The disciples can't do this simple thing. These fishermen can't sail to the fishing town.

A storm comes up, they row against the wind and waves all night, and finally they're about to sink and drown. Here are twelve strong and successful fishermen, who can't do the one thing they've been trained to do: sail a boat and get fish. It's as if Christ is saying, "It's not about your skills, your training, or the economy around you, boys. It's about putting your trust not in what you know, but in who you know. So the next time I ask you to feed the folks, give them all that you have and don't worry about how you'll feed yourselves."

I gave up fishing a long time ago. I learned when I was around eight that it was easier to buy a fish dinner than catch a fish dinner and, for me, buying dinner was a whole lot more fun. But that evening in Pat's boat in Oriental harbor I caught a glimpse of the joy of fishing. I mean, I was catching fish! Lots of them. In fact, I was on my way to catching a whole boatload of those rascals when Pat suddenly grabbed the light out of my hand and made me stop. I guess Pat wasn't into fishing like I was. But that's okay. At least this year when the Saltwater Fish-a-Thon folks come calling I'll have a story to tell them.

"Yes sir, I caught me some fish last year. How many? Why, at least three . . . . No, didn't use any live bait, just a flashlight. That's right, a flashlight. Well, the thing is, those fish jumped right in my boat . . . . Yessir, they jumped right in. Craziest thing you ever — Hello? Hello?"

"Hey, honey, will you check the caller ID? That nice fellow from the Division of Marine Fisheries got cut off and I didn't get a chance to finish telling him my fishing story."

➤ **Hard Aground hint:** Give a man a fish, and you'll feed him for a day. Teach a man to fish, and he will sit in a boat and listen to country music all afternoon.

➤ **Passage markers:** *But so that we may not offend them, go to the lake and throw out your line. Take the first fish you catch; open its mouth and you will find a four-drachma coin. Take it and give it to them for my tax and yours.* —Matthew 17:27. For further inspiration read John 21:1–14.

➤ **Prayer focus:** Those trying to catch fish, catch up on their bills, or just trying to catch a break in life.

10

A Force to be Wreck'ned With

SOMETIMES WHEN THE ANCHOR IS SET AND THE SUNDOWNERS ARE SERVED, the anticipated arrival at some delightful destination can be anticlimactic. There are days when sand fleas, Jet Skis, and fast-moving northerlies splatter the Kodak moment with just enough graffiti to render the carefully colored canvas unsuitable for framing. On days like this, I delete the mental moment, forgetting that it ever happened. "What's done is done and no amount of spilled milk is going to make it any butter," my buddy Joe used to say. Joe spouted puns by the gross.

On the day we arrived at Cape Lookout the crew of *Kontigo* breathed a silent thank-you that our Mercury Force 9.9 had run so well. Motoring the thirty-some miles from Oriental isn't normally a big deal, but I had spent the better part of a year repairing my Force 9.9 outboard in hopes of taking just such a trip, and now that the bow was nudged up close to the edge of the low-tide line I wanted to savor the moment. My friend Pat and I unfolded a pair of frayed Wal-Mart lawn chairs, planted them on the roof of my old trimaran, and watched the wind strum the strands of sea oats glistening in the summer sun. The August heat baked the soft sand, searing the soles of tender feet and forcing a covey of barefoot children to sprint along the water's edge with outstretched arms as they mimicked the sea gulls soaring overhead. It was the perfect period to a long passage.

The second long swallow of my cold Corona was interrupted by one of my boys asking, "Hey, will you take us over to East Beach so we can go surfing?"

I was tired of the tinny twang of an outboard and I didn't have the energy or inclination to mount Pat's old four-horsepower Johnson on the dinghy, so I looked towards Pat for support.

"Guys, why don't you swim some more," Pat countered. "The *Bomba Shack* will be here in a few minutes and Dan will probably have some cheese and crackers and chips and stuff. You know how that crew always has plenty of good food."

The rations on *Kontigo* usually consist of pretzels, Pop-Tarts, and water, so our boys welcomed this anticipated buffet of unauthorized contraband and ceased their talk of surfing. When the last of the Corona was sloshing about at the bottom of the bottle, the *Bomba Shack* pulled alongside to raft up. I wedged a creosote-stained fender between the two hulls and welcomed them to the Bight.

"My crew wants to go over to East Beach," Dan said, looking down at the black stain from my boat fender, "so if you'll give me a minute I'll launch my inflatable so we can all dinghy over together."

I told my boys our plans had changed, that we'd get those snacks later, and to get their surfboards ready. Dan pulled the starter on his new Yamaha outboard. It spit and sputtered and stopped. Dan primed the pump and tried again, this time with less success. I put down my surfboard. Within minutes Pat and Dan had the cover off, the spark plug removed, and a mess of tools scattered about the floor of Dan's inflatable. The girls on *Bomba Shack* had returned to their beach towels to spread another layer of tanning oil on Dan's non-skid deck, and my boys had found the cheese and crackers.

Now there's one thing you can say about Pat. He loves a challenge almost as much as Dan loves to have his stuff working right, so between the two of them they were a force to be wreck'ned with. They worked on that outboard for almost an hour. But at the end of the day, the Yamaha reigned supreme and we remained stuck on the hook.

"If you don't know how to cuss, an outboard will teach you," Dan said, putting his broken Yamaha back on the stern rail of *Bomba Shack*. We put Pat's four-horse Johnson on my dinghy and, with my boys and surfboards, went waddling across the bight at five knots towards East Beach.

Later that night, as both crews swapped dinner morsels and drinks under a full moon, I thought about how cruising brings folks of all social classes together. Rich and poor share the same anchorage, the same dreams, and many times the same technology. The only real difference seems to be the experience of the crew, the size of the toys, and the age of the tools that keep it all afloat. In Dan's case, he had a brand-new fancy outboard that wouldn't run. I had an older-model Force 9.9 that, while temperamental, had powered us to a perfect summer sunset. Pat had a thirty-year-old motor that only had one speed — slow — but it always started on the second pull. Each outboard reflected our determination to be cruising and a certain income level.

Part of the joy of cruising is meeting people of diverse occupations and backgrounds, and becoming fast friends because of a shared interest in sailing. I hardly ever spend time with my boating buddies during the long, cold months of winter. I take these slipmates for granted, assuming they'll be at the dock beside me when I return next season. Most are — but occasionally I'll discover that one has moved to another marina, gone cruising for good, or swallowed the anchor, sold the boat, and moved in with the kids. I ought to take more care with the docklines that bind us together, but I don't. Boating buddies deserve better than this.

Our cruising friends see us at our worst and accept us anyway. When we sail into heavy seas and begin to hurl over the rail, our friends sit upwind with a damp cloth and averted eyes, knowing from past experience that pride, modesty, and greasy foods are best left ashore. When my crew rises early, they usually find me on a bunk in the salon, drooling on my pillow with my mouth agape like a stupid grouper. If I go to the head while they gather for breakfast, my business becomes their business and if I wish to have any crew next time, I will open the deck hatch and use the air freshener when I exit. Do cruising companions mind these close quarters and intense inspections of hygiene and personal habits? Not at all. Most feel it's a small price to pay for companionship at sea.

No matter what the passage, whether short or long, we're all just passing from one age to the next, growing older and weaker and, sometimes, wiser. The smart ones know that friends and family are the lubricant that makes the tough moments easier to endure. Those who bring sunshine into our lives cannot keep it to themselves, and when you find a friend like that, you know it's a gift from God. Boating seems to breed these kinds of buddies. Perhaps it's the exposure to other cultures, to the raw elements of nature, or to the admission that none of us has all the answers but we each have something to share, some unique quality that makes us special. Boating buddies seem eager to help us grin and shine, and wipe away the tears during the tough times. I feel fortunate to have found so many during my years on the water.

The next morning the *Bomba Shack* raised her sails and disappeared towards Beaufort with Dan's crew of lovely ladies lounging on the bow. We hooted and waved at Dan's boat as he sailed out into the ocean, hoping to fall in behind his wake. But our wild cheers turn to wailing when my own outboard spit and sputtered and stopped. As we sat dead in the water, the current cast us towards the shoals along the edge of the channel. With my crew standing in knee-deep surf, pushing us back towards the channel, Pat mounted his old Johnson on my boat's stern, pulled the rope twice, and pointed the bow towards home. We were almost thirty miles from our marina on a thirty-foot trimaran, with a thirty-year-old four-horsepower outboard motoring us into the ocean. The only things we had going for us were a sunny sky, the heat of the day, and our friendship.

We cleared the Bight at Cape Lookout a little before noon but didn't enter the mouth of Core Creek until almost dusk. It had taken us almost five hours to make the three-hour journey, and we were only halfway home. We motored up the Intracoastal Waterway that evening, illuminating the channel markers with spotlights. We were hungry and tired, but excited at the prospect of a hot meal at M & M's, so at a quarter to ten I called Marsha to tell her we were almost in Oriental harbor. She explained that the restaurant would be closing in fifteen minutes. My crew would go hungry another evening. But there is more to life than food for the belly — there is nourishment that comes from committed friends and the shared pain of suffering that binds us together.

As I hung up the phone we motored across the flat waters of the Neuse with the final full moon of the summer painting the river in shades of silver and I offered a silent thanks to God for old friends with old outboards who share my love for sailing old sailboats. Where two or more are gathered together, friends are a force to be wreck'ned with, and we were that night. And we will be again.

▶ **Hard Aground hint:** Prosperity makes friends and adversity tries them. To find out which kind of friends you have, take them sailing.

▶ **Passage markers:** *I no longer call you servants, because a servant does not know his master's business. Instead, I have called you friends, for everything that I learned from my Father I have made known to you.* —John 15:15. For further inspiration read Luke 10:30–37.

▶ **Prayer focus:** Friendships that have been neglected and need forgiveness and restoration.

11

Oscar Mired Dinners

FOR TEN DOLLARS WE GOT ONE OF THE FINEST SEAFOOD DINNERS THE Lowcountry could offer and an evening of entertainment that has lasted a lifetime.

It was Rick's idea, really. He was the captain's kid and we figured that if the prank seemed too daring for his old man, Rick would take the fall for the rest of us. He didn't, but that's the way we figured it. By the time Rick finked on Lin and I, fingering us for the petty pirates that we were, the escapade had grown to legendary proportions and everyone wanted to be numbered among the band of buccaneers. But for now, it was Rick's idea. I was just the guy driving the boat.

Lin was the navigator, and it was his job to keep us clear of the shoals and mud flats of Georgia's Sea Islands. Our passage up the Intracoastal Waterway from Jacksonville, Florida, had been plagued by swift currents, slow days, and the gradual acceptance that life around these sea islands moved with the ebb and flow of the tidal times. Fish and fowl and boat all moved along to the same slow pulse of the gravitational pull.

Our adventure had begun earlier that morning with the wind ripping through the sun-dried sawgrass of a tidal marsh, thrashing the restless reeds in advance of a summer squall. The morning blossomed with the passing shower, and soon the narrow river swelled beyond the channel markers, washing over oyster beds and cautious crabs in a relentless march for the high-tide line.

Somewhere up ahead, beyond the next turn or the one after that, was a fork in the waterway called Hell's Gate. Rick's dad, Oscar, had warned us to stay alert for this navigational nightmare and to watch for the set of range markers. The symbolism of the topography and the mischief we would propose should have been a harbinger of things to come, but we were young and stupid and blinded by our faith in two forgiving fathers — Rick's dad and my heavenly one.

In Rick's case, his dad was down below mulling over the waterway charts and making plans for another dull meal aboard ship. I didn't know it at the time — but was about to learn — that Oscar had this thing about Dinty Moore beef stew. He considered this canned hash to be an integral part of the cruising experience. All I could envision was the regurgitated heap of cold beef hash from my days as a Boy Scout. I hoped Oscar's loud boasting of fresh stew was for show and to scare us, but Rick assured me it was not.

"My old man loves the stuff," he said.

"You're kidding. How can he eat something that looks and smells like canned dog food?"

"Oh, it's not so bad if you add a little wine to it," Rick offered. "The trick is to drown it thoroughly in merlot while Dad's out in the cockpit checking the channel markers. If you doctor it up enough, by the time you've finished a bowl you've got a little buzz and are tempted to go back for seconds. But don't let that wine high fool you. Stop at one helping or you'll pay for it in the morning."

Well, I had never had a beef stew hangover and didn't care to try one that far from central plumbing, so I asked Rick if there was another option.

"Crabs."

"Crabs?" I asked. "You mean like stopping for a crab dinner along the waterway?"

"No, I mean like grabbing one of these traps we keep passing and boiling a few."

"What's your dad gonna say?" Lin asked.

"I'm not sure. It's hard to guess which way he'll come down on something like that. But right now it's crabs or Dinty Moore and I'm willing to try a little larceny if y'all are."

Like I said, Lin and I figured Rick had a better feel for his dad's tempera-ment than we did, so we found a false sense of security in Rick's courage.

Along the Southern coast, locals still set shrimp nets and crab traps in small creeks and tidal pools, preserving a way of life that is fighting to stay ahead of the kudzu creep of four-lane causeways and back-nine bunkers. Motoring north along the waterway, we tried to ignore the rumble of rubber tires on steel girders overhead, because off to port a broad savanna stretched beyond the back lawn of a plantation home.

"Do you think we're close to Hell's Gate?" I asked as the channel nar-rowed.

"Not sure," Rick replied. "We'll know for certain when we get to the next marker."

None of us had thought to check the tide, but then no one had consid-ered the penalty for poaching crabs either. As accomplished sinners we didn't need to be led into temptation. We could find it on our own just fine. While Lin and Rick gathered their tools for our evening heist, Oscar was down below banging on a steel pan to warn us that preparations for dinner were underway. Together we clung to the hope that soon the Styrofoam float we craved so des-perately would drift into view and spare us another dull meal aboard Oscar's boat. What had begun as a lukewarm alliance to poaching crabs now possessed our very soul, and we were rabid with the prospect of a fresh seafood dinner.

"It's tough when you want to steal and can't," Rick mumbled after a few minutes of searching the dusk-darkened waters.

"Or mercy," I thought.

Just as Oscar announced that he'd found the can opener, Lin's light illuminated a beige float bobbing off the port side. Rick rushed forward to get into position while I carefully steered us away from the main channel and towards dinner. I was reluctant to throttle down for fear of alerting Oscar of our intentions, so I watched and waited and hoped our brief diversion from course would go unnoticed. Rick knelt down, wedging his head beneath the lifelines to lie flat on the narrow side deck. I was watching Rick reach over and down towards the water to snag the trap, when suddenly I saw Lin twist and stumble on the bow, his thigh landing hard against the bow pulpit. I only had a moment to wonder at this before I, too, succumbed to a rush of vertigo as the cockpit floor rose beneath me in that sickening manner that accompanies a grounding.

"What's going on up there?" Oscar shouted, charging up the companion-way. "I thought I told you guys to call me if you weren't sure where the channel was."

He was standing in the cockpit with a half-opened can of Dinty Moore in one hand and a plastic spatula in the other.

"Rick, you should know better than this. Rick? Where's Rick?"

"Down here."

We looked off the stern and saw Rick standing in the water beside the dinghy.

"What are you doing down there, son?"

"I fell in."

"Well, if you can stand up, then you know dang well this isn't where the boat's supposed to be. Get in the dinghy and take the anchor out into the main channel. Eddie, you get ready to winch it in. Y'all better pray that the tide is rising."

It wasn't.

I learned that night that the secret to life is enjoying the passing of tides. It's a hard lesson to learn. You learn it on a shoal or you learn it bucking a current, but in the end you come to appreciate the power of the tides. It is the eternal flow of highs and lows that sets the pace of life. Fish and fowl and fair-weather sailors all float along on the same river of ups and downs.

Our plans for tomorrow become the broken dreams of the past, and the trials and tough times shape us in ways pleasant circumstances never can. It's during those times when we're spiritually stuck that God's grace is revealed in full — when his light shines brightest, illuminating our path back towards him. He has set the boundaries for our safe passage by providing us with his precepts.

"Oh, how I love your law," says the psalmist. "I meditate on it all day long.

Your commands make me wiser than my enemies. . . . . I have more insight than all my teachers, for I meditate on your statutes. . . . Your word is a lamp to my feet and a light for my path."

I knew a little of God's law that evening as we cruised the skinny waters of Georgia. I knew stealing was wrong, but I didn't protest too loudly. I thought it would be okay that one time. It was not. It is through small steps that we wander away from God. We indulge in the small sin of petty theft, find it filling and almost harmless, and then move on towards grander larceny. Men sneak a look down a woman's blouse, call it casual lust, and then slide into adultery. Women comment on a friend's character flaw, call it constructive criticism, and then proceed to gossip about her. Sin is never satisfied. It always wants more, craves a richer experience, because it ultimately wants all of you. There is no harmless sin, no victimless sin, because each sin destroys a little more of who we were meant to be. And it separates us from God.

But it sure was fun, for a time, that night as we stole those crabs.

We convinced Oscar that since we'd gone to the trouble of running aground, we might as well enjoy a crab feast. Rick pulled the chicken-wire cage on board and we dumped ten or more of the frightened critters into a pot of boiling water. I was pleased to see that their spastic convulsions stopped almost as soon as they hit the water. Moments later we were sitting around the table dipping chucks of beefy white meat into bowls of golden butter and listening to Oscar's tales of other waterway trips. The stories and crabs kept coming, each nourishing us in different ways, and when we were finished Oscar added another to his collection.

"Y'all chip in a few dollars while I write a note."

We glanced at each other, puzzled at his request, but did as ordered. Oscar went into the head and dug through his dock kit and returned with an aspirin bottle. He emptied the pills on the counter, then rolled the money and note together and slipped them into the bottle.

"I plan to be gone tomorrow morning when that fisherman comes back for his trap. He's gonna be pretty ticked off to find it's empty except for this aspirin bottle. Ten dollars ain't much, but maybe it will make up for what we took. Could be it's more than he would've made off them anyway. In any case, these crabs and this grounding will give us something to talk about the rest of the trip."

And it still does.

➤ **Hard Aground hint:** The only way to avoid mistakes is to gain experience, and the only way to gain experience is to make mistakes. It seems to me that a boat is the ultimate classroom.

➤ **Passage markers:** *But God demonstrates his own love for us in this: While we were still sinners, Christ died for us.* —Romans 5:8. For further inspiration read Romans 6:23.

➤ **Prayer focus:** If you are spiritually stuck, return to the guidebook and meditate on God's word.

12

Signal Flags

BEFORE RADIO, THE ONLY WAY TO COMMUNICATE SHIP-TO-SHIP OR ship-to-shore was with rocks. The caller, usually a tiller-marketer from another vessel, would toss a rock to get the crew's attention and then the man — but sometimes the woman — would pick up the rock and throw it back. Conversations of this nature would go on for hours, sometimes for days, as the two boats circled each other before one of the crew would toss all their rocks in the air to indicate that they didn't have a clue what the other party was saying. This would cause the boat to capsize, since rocks served not only as vital communication's equipment but also as ballast. (Even early in their development cycle rocks were proving that they could multitask.) But placing a call with rocks proved to be a very ineffective method for sending a message, since oftentimes a rock would strike one party in the head, thus abruptly ending the conversation. Today we refer to this as a "dropped call."

Then flags were invented. Flags quickly replaced rocks on ships. In fact, pennant flags were so much easier to use that people everywhere began using them. You may even have some on your boat. So how might one use a flag at sea, you may ask?

Let's say you're the skipper of a military transport vessel in charge of a secret mission to start a war with another country and you want to send a signal to the rest of the fleet that you need to stop and take a potty break. Well, you would use two identical flags, each with the letter P, to spell the phrase, P P, which in flag code means "Keep well clear of me." These are big military transport vessels we're talking about here, and you don't want to be around when they open their holding tanks.

Or let's say you're a Latin American diplomat transporting vital and highly addictive, not to mention expensive, cargo and you want to warn other diplomats in your fleet that the U.S. Coast Guard has set up a routine safety inspection at the off-ramp to Miami. Well you'd use two flags spelling the phrase S O to indicate to everyone in your caravan that they should "stop immediately!" Then you would follow this broadcast with D V, the international code for "I am drifting." In this case you would, in fact, be drifting towards the Bahamas, which would be a good thing since you could then take the back roads through the Abacos and re-emerge on the express ramp at the Gulf Stream. As you can tell all of this flag stuff is really important if you're heading to work, war, or the bathroom.

That's why the Organization of Letter Carriers, the group that controls A, E, I, O, U, and sometimes Y and W, took it upon themselves to come up with the International Code of Signals. The International Code of Signals, known within the tiller communications industry as flag codes, adopted twenty-six code flags, which just happens to be the number of letters in the alphabet. There are also nine numeral flags, three repeater flags, and an answering pennant flag that goes to voice mail after four rings.

Suppose you want to call your dad. Well, you would raise the code flag P for Papa. Or let's say it was your day off and you wanted to take a break from scrubbing decks and play a little golf. You'd hoist the code flag G for Golf, followed by W for Whiskey. After whiskey, you could raise the code flag F for Foxtrot, but only if you really felt frisky. As you can see, flag codes are way better than plain old rocks.

Even Moses took to using signal flags. When he wanted to build an altar, he started with some old rocks and called it, "The Lord is my Banner." We don't know if God liked being a banner, but the next day when the Amalekites attacked Israel, Moses stood on the hill and raised his staff, and Joshua's men began to whip up on the Amalekites. As long as Moses held up his banner on the stick, the Israelites won, but whenever he lowered his hands, they would lose.

Because Moses was really old and the Wave hadn't been invented yet, some of his men put some stones under him to support his stick, and that's why today we call employees of a large company "the staff." This is also why banners are really popular in sporting arenas when a team or nation wants to honor a great victory or championship.

But enough of the flag basics. Sometimes you want to engage in complex discussions that involve multiple words, and that's where it's helpful to have a second semester of code flag. We call this course Code Flag 102. In Code Flag 102 you master the use of — and this is where it gets tricky — two flags. As a good rule of thumb or forefinger, two flags hoisted simultaneously indicate a vessel that is in distress or executing a maneuver or crew member.

For example: A C means "I am abandoning my vessel." You would see this, perhaps, after a week in August at Cape Lookout on a sailboat without air conditioning. We've already covered S O and D V, so we won't repeat ourselves except to say that D V does not mean dive boat. A dive boat is required to show flag code Alpha on a rigid panel, but they often skip this rule and use an unofficial flag with a red field and white cross. We don't know why this is. There are other things we don't know which we'll cover later.

And now that it is later we'll discuss those things we don't understand. Why does a ship at dock run up the so-called "Blue Peter" flag (actually code flag Papa) to indicate that the ship is preparing to sail? Hmm?? And why is a ship arriving in port required to fly Quebec, which is commonly called the quarantine flag, even though hardly anyone ever sails to Quebec anymore? And finally, what do three, four, five, six and seven flag signals have in common? The answer is that they each have additional meanings at the international level but we don't know what they are.

Which brings us to Code Flag 103, which is so called because it meets in Room 103. Code Flag 103 covers military flag codes, which are different from just regular flag codes because, well, they just are. For instance, code flag India flown on a U.S. warship means "I'm coming alongside"; however, to a merchant or pleasure vessel it means "I'm altering my course to port and outsourcing your job." To avoid this confusion, warships use the Answering Pennant code flag as the top flag when communicating with merchant vessels. In this way the other ships know which dialect the ship is speaking. Confusing? You bet, and that's why warships also carry really big rocket launchers. Because nothing cuts through the confusion of code flag fatigue faster than rocklike bombs striking the water off your bow. In any language, no matter where you're from this means it's time to stop, run up the white flag, and take a potty break.

And so I will. But before I go let me just say that if you have learned anything about code flags and their importance in piloting your vessel, I apologize. It certainly was not my intent to enlighten or educate.

➤ **Hard Aground hint:** Anything worth taking seriously is worth making fun of. —Anonymous

➤ **Passage markers:** *Then the Lord said to Moses, "Write this on a scroll as something to be remembered and make sure that Joshua hears it, because I will completely blot out the memory of Amalek from under heaven." Moses built an altar and called it The Lord is my Banner.* —Exodus 17:14–15. For further inspiration read Matthew 26:36–45.

➤ **Prayer focus:** Those who feel their prayers aren't being answered or their call is being dropped.

Every few minutes I'd poke my head into the cockpit to make sure the autopilot was still automatically taking us off course, and to see if Bennie had fallen over or jumped in. During one of these inspections, I brought her lunch on a plastic plate and asked, "Do you want to eat this sandwich yourself, or should I just throw it over the side and save you the trouble?"

Part III

Not a Yacht Happening in My Slip: Boats Slip-Sliding Away

13

Let's Go to 68

TODAY WE'RE GOING TO EXPLORE THE OFTEN NEGLECTED AND completely confusing role transmissions play in cruising. Because my friend Dave is stranded in Green Turtle Cay with major transmission problems, we will use him as an example of how neglecting your transmission can ruin a perfectly good cruise and—

Oops! Silly me. I didn't finish reading the last part of my writing assignment. It seems my editor wants me to address the subject of ship-to-ship transmissions, not shifting gear transmissions on your boat's engine. With that in mind let's begin our discussion with a few observations.

Each morning, when I arise, I tune my VHF radio to the weather station. Listening to NOAA's weather forecast for the coming day is a wonderful source of entertainment. The weather synopsis for my area is always succinct and clear and sometimes even accurate, but the best part is the way it's only concerned with my little corner of paradise. I like comparing the reported wave heights at remote sea buoys with what I'm seeing on the beach, in the hopes I can derive some sort of formula by which to predict surf conditions. You know, eight- to ten-foot seas off Diamond Shoals equals four-foot surf at Shackleford Banks. It's a tribal surfer character flaw I can't shake. The NOAA weather radio broadcasts for our area used to originate out of New Bern, North Carolina. Back then the voice on the other end of the speaker sounded as friendly and sincere as a Motel 6 commercial, but sometime in the 1990s, when Congress was passing another pay increase for itself, the government reduced funding and moved the NOAA office to Newport, North Carolina. Now we have a computer-generated voice delivering a monotone summary of impending natural disasters. I'm sure this is less expensive and a more efficient use of our tax dollars, but a hurricane warning issued by Hal the Computer Voice just doesn't have the same urgency and inflection as a real person about to lose his house to a storm surge.

By far the most exciting aspect of listening to my VHF radio is chasing other conversations up the dial. The tenor of the discussion changes depending on the day of the week and the neighborhood I'm visiting, but a typical report sounds like the frenzied activity I heard this morning.

Someone is reporting that the crew of *Tide One On* is still recovering from last night's festivities at M & M's and probably won't depart for Cape Lookout until lunch or later, which is fine with the rest of the fleet since *Tide One On*'s crew is a rowdy bunch anyway. The skipper of *Carpe Diem Wit*, which must be Latin for "seize the idiot," has agreed to serve as the committee boat for Sunday's race because he has the horn and stopwatch and is the only one other than last week's winner who understands the starting times. *Breaking Wind* thinks that the microphone might be off the hook on *Disconnected* because no one is responding to his call for a ride to breakfast. The skipper of *Impetuous* may or may not sail to Ocracoke, depending on the conditions out in the Pamlico Sound, and no one is surprised at this since we haven't seen him with his sails up in over a year. The crew of *Pete and Re-Pete* is planning to attend the Beaufort Bash in the harbor unless they run aground exiting Core Creek. We think they will, since they usually do.

When I bought my first boat and began listening to the personal conversations of other boaters I felt guilty. It seemed like I was eavesdropping. All that changed, however, when I ran aground off Ocracoke the first time. The morning after our midnight grounding I called the Coast Guard on channel 16 to see if they would tow us off a shoal that had wandered into my keel. They asked me to use channel 21 as my working channel, since they were working and I wasn't. Every few hours they would call on 21 to ask, "Are you still in your previous location?"

"Yep, we're still stuck," I'd say.

"What is the condition of the crew?"

"Oh, we're fine. I'm playing dominoes with my son and he's winning."

"Well, if anything changes give us a call."

"Like if I win a game?"

"No, like if you get your vessel floating again."

I didn't think much about these terse conversations until I was safely moored at the public docks later that afternoon, and bragging to a crowd of new cruising friends about our misadventure.

"Oh, so you're the guy who was aground outside the channel."

"Yep, that was me. Why, did you pass us when you came in?" I asked.

"Nah, we were listening in on 21 when you were talking to the Coast Guard. Was that your first time?"

"What? Sailing to Ocracoke and coming down that channel?"

"No, playing dominoes."

"Oh, that. No, I'm afraid not. My son is as good at dominoes as I am bad at reading a chart."

"I gathered as much."

Intercessory prayer can be a little like the VHF radio. We can listen to the needs of others, hear the stress in their voice, and know without asking that we need to lift them up in prayer. Last week I was at the grocery store discussing dinner preparations with the clerk in the checkout lane when she told me that day was her mom's birthday. I said I hoped her mother had a wonderful birthday dinner.

"She's not doing too good," the young girl said. "She's in the hospital." As I walked to my car I keyed the mic and offered an arrow prayer. I have another friend who, before he says grace in a restaurant, makes it a habit of asking his waitress if there's anything she would like him to pray for. Several times he's found himself holding the hand of a stranger he'll never see again, praying out loud for a problem that is foreign to him but dear to the one who's silently crying in the booth beside him. Christ said that where two or more were gathered together, he would be with them. If we want healing and help we should have fewer pity parties and more prayer time together.

When it comes to interceding for our slipmates, however, we don't even need to ask for permission. We only have to be willing to violate the privacy rights of those using the public airwaves by listening in on their conversations. With that in mind let's look at the correct use of a VHF radio. Here's a list of rules sanctioned by the United States Power Squadron, with some general observations added that I think you'll find useful. Many of these tips can be applied to your prayer life as well.

• Monitor channel 16 whenever your radio is on unless you are transmitting. (If you are transmitting, monitor your speech, because almost everyone else is monitoring channel 16.)

• Identify your vessel at the beginning and ending of each transmission. (This helps others know who was stupid enough to run aground at the edge of the channel. Or you can do like me and avoid detection by identifying yourself as another vessel.)

• Use channel 16 or 9 for hailing another vessel, and when contact is made shift to a working channel. (I use 68 but you may prefer another channel. In any case you should scan the working channel first to make sure there aren't other conversations already in progress that are more spirited and controversial than what you are preparing to offer.)

• Use your radio's low-power setting whenever practical, especially in the harbor. (This is easy to do on my boat because my battery is always dead or dying. On your radio, you may need to manually activate this feature.)

• Always speak slowly and distinctly, and do not shout. (This suggestion is mainly intended for those born and reared in northern climates where everyone speaks like the legal disclaimer guy on a car commercial.)

• Use channel 13 when trying to communicate with a bridge tender. (This is the official method for initiating a conversation, but blowing a horn, calling on your cell phone, or tossing rocks at the window may work faster.)

• Keep all communications brief, and avoid cursing. (Save that form of seasoned communication for the boatyard when you're told that your transmission will need to be rebuilt.)

• Finally, remember that boat means Break Out Another Thousand, so stop complaining to everyone on the airwaves about how much it's going to cost to get the clutch plate repaired on your transmission, and pray instead that the yard doesn't find even more problems that need repairing. You've got a boat and you're cruising, for crying out loud. You didn't expect to be rich too, did you?

➤ **Hard Aground hint:** Don't say nasty things on the airways, or harbor mean thoughts about others. There is rarely enough space on a boat to carry both a grudge and crew, so pack shorts and a smile and wear them often.

➤ **Passage markers:** *Is any one of you in trouble? He should pray. Is anyone happy? Let him sing songs of praise. Is any one of you sick? He should call the elders of the church to pray over him and anoint him with oil in the name of the Lord. And the prayer offered in faith will make the sick person well; the Lord will raise him up. If he has sinned, he will be forgiven. Therefore confess your sins to each other and pray for each other so that you may be healed. The prayer of a righteous man is powerful and effective.* —James 5:13–16. For further inspiration read Matthew 26:36–45.

➤ **Prayer focus:** Those reluctant to share their needs with others, ask for help, or seek prayers.

14

New Boat? I Wooden Have One

I WANT A WOODEN SAILBOAT. I DON'T NEED A WOODEN SAILBOAT, DON'T need to be told I don't need a wooden sailboat, and don't care if you have a wooden-boat disaster story. If you want to talk me out of buying a wooden boat, don't waste your time. I'm in heat and I'm not listening.

For some years now I've suffered from a carnal attraction to low-slung vessels trimmed in shades of ivory with petite, inverted sterns. This juvenile desire is not some sudden flight of fancy that's overwhelmed my sanity now that I'm between boats, because I craved wooden boats even as I cruised on the fiberglass float we call a sailboat. I can't prove that lusting after another boat is a sin, but it probably should be.

Wooden boats recall a time when watercraft were built for vocation, not vacation, so try as I might, I can't help but look and leer when I see one sailing up our creek. Last summer, as I was anchored in Ocracoke riding out a vicious thunderstorm that was moving along the edge of a frisky cold front, a slender Hinckley 28 came tacking across the shoals beyond the end of the channel. I watched the boat work its way past the markers until it turned into Silver Lake and began maneuvering through the crowded fleet. The skipper selected a spot just a little north of my bow, then turned into the wind and released the jib sheet. Running forward, he leaned over the bowsprit and flipped a clevis pin on the bow roller, then stood over the bow chock as the galvanized chain fell down and away into the dark water. When the boat began to stumble backwards under the vigor of the freshening breeze, he pulled the boom across the deck and backwinded the main sail. He lashed the boom to a cleat and then walked back to the cockpit, grabbed the tiller, and guided the stern downwind towards my boat. Just as it looked as if he would impale himself on our bow, the anchor buried itself in the mud and jerked the bow into the wind like a spirited mare coming up short. The boat stopped, and all I could hear was the slapping sound of the mainsail beating the varnish off the wooden mast. All in all, it was quite a performance, and I said so as I rowed over to congratulate him.

"A feat like that deserves a cold drink," I said, offering him one from my cooler.

"I could use a bilge pump instead," he said, standing up in the companionway. "I'm sinking."

"You serious?"

"Yeah, I have about six inches of water down here and it's still pouring in. I got caught in that storm and lost my bearings at the entrance to the channel. I must have missed the marker because I hit a shoal and the keel took a real pounding before I tacked over and bounced her off. I think she might have cracked a rib. The bilge overflowed, shorting out the battery. I can't crank the engine or run the bilge pump. It wasn't too bad as long as I was moving, but now that I've stopped she's filling up fast. I need to get to a dock with electricity so I can get the pump going."

I rowed back to my boat and called the Coast Guard on channel 16. They hurried along and towed my friend over to the public docks, bringing a crowd of onlookers as they did. When I stopped by a few hours later to check on him, the boat was spitting out more water than it was sucking in, and he was pretty sure it wasn't going to sink. I took one last look at the mess of oil, sea water, and clothing littering the cabin floor and then walked around the harbor to get some ice cream.

Now you'd think that a guy who runs aground as often as I do would be reluctant to own a boat that can splinter and break apart on a submerged shoal, but I'm not. The first thing I did when I got back to Oriental that Sunday was to grab the latest copy of *Wooden Boat* magazine and scan the classic boats section for a deal on a Hinckley. In case you don't know, there are no deals on

Hinckleys and probably never will be. But that doesn't keep me from looking and lusting anyway. Each winter I staple a new *Wooden Boat* calendar to the walls of my study, and if there's a particularly gorgeous spread one month, I'll remove the staples and slide the picture into the bottom drawer of my desk.

My wife surprised me on my birthday a few years back and gave me a framed picture of one of the prints I'd collected. It was a simple shot of a small, open-cockpit sailboat — a working skiff rigged with a cotton sail that was loosely lashed to the varnished boom lying across the gunwales. The boat was resting on a sandy spit somewhere in the Bahamas, and the mast stood out against the Windex sky of a sunny day. Every so often I look up from my keyboard and study that picture, pretending the skipper has wandered beyond the edge of the print towards the deeper water of the reef where dinner awaits beneath a coral head. It's a simple boat for a simple man, and simply something I mean to own someday.

I have a friend who's building a wooden boat in his garage. I can't build a hatch board, much less a boat, but I think there would be a great deal of satisfaction in constructing a vessel into which you plan to consign your life. A boat that can carry you to your death or carry you to paradise has a certain power that a homemade wooden bench never can.

That's why I'm looking for a small wooden boat with a sturdy trunk. Something with character and cleats and just enough rot to keep my boys and me busy sanding and caulking through the winter. I would never attempt to build a boat by hand, but I think there is great value in maintaining a wooden boat and passing it on to the kids and grandkids. It would be their summer sloop — their dream machine docked behind their grandparents' Lake Norman home. A vessel on which they could learn basic seamanship and navigation while Bennie and I perfected our search-and-rescue techniques. Once I was certain they weren't going to sink or drown I would encourage them to sail over to Tom Sawyer Island and spend the evening camping on Pirate Hill as the bonfire off Injun Joe Point faded in the cool of a fall evening. I think my boys would take a lot of pride in caring for and sailing a wooden boat like this. I know I would.

In his letter to the church in Ephesus, Paul says we are God's "workmanship" — a work of art shaped by and for him. Some days I feel as though I'm sprawled across his workbench, looking down at the shavings he's whittled away from my life — the faults, failures, and disappointments. With carving and shaping comes the pain of perfection administered by the hands of a master carpenter. Sometimes I find that what I thought was my strength, was just an old knot — the remnants of a dead branch that had to be cut away. My desire should be to give myself over to him, to trust that he'll shape me into a thing of beauty. A classic, if you will.

Each day in some small way he calls me to let go of my past and embrace the future. The more I let him sand and slice, the more truly myself I become. I may never own a wooden boat, but I know perfection when I see it. God has promised each of us that if we'll but give our life to Christ, we will become a work of art. I, for one, "wooden" want it any other way.

➤ **Hard Aground hint:** Whatever you do that God has called you to do is sacred work.

➤ **Passage markers:** *Consider it pure joy, my brothers, whenever you face trials of many kinds, because you know that the testing of your faith develops perseverance. Perseverance must finish its work so that you may be mature and complete, not lacking anything.* —James 1:2–4. For further guidance read Ephesians 2:1–10.

➤ **Prayer focus:** Those who know there is more to life than living and would like to be shaped into the image of God to be used for his purposes.

15

Cockpit Downsizing

POVERTY IS A HECK OF A HANDICAP FOR A GUY PRONE TO CHRONIC CRUISING. I'm ashamed to admit that a few years back I tried to reverse my life of destitution by attending a motivational, get-rich-quick seminar held in the cramped conference room of an Interstate motel that was hygienically challenged. The propaganda in the brochure guaranteed that vast sums of money would flow into my pockets if I would only follow the five principles outlined in their program. I was assured that I would be the first in my territory to share in this business opportunity, so I filled out my name tag and went along with the program, responding to their questions like every other dolt in the room.

"Would you like to make a lot of money in a short time?" the speaker asked.

Yes, I answered.

"Do you enjoy working long hours for almost no money?" I was distracted by a tray of doughnuts, so I answered in the affirmative and got this one wrong. These classes move quickly, so you have pay close attention.

"Do you have numerous friends and relatives who could benefit from these products and services?" No. I gave the wrong answer again. They expected me to have friends and family. I would have to work on this area.

"Do you make all the money you want today in your present job?" No. Got this one right.

"Are you willing to invest a small amount of money to begin your journey to financial freedom?"

Well, there was the rub. I didn't have any money. At least not in the sum they were asking for. If I did have that kind of money, I thought, I wouldn't be sitting in a hot hotel along Interstate 95 trying to find a way to get rich quick. It seemed to me they would have known this from my interest in their seminar and I said so rather loudly. The speaker didn't appreciate my frank appraisal of his business proposal, however, so he ordered me out of the room and off the property. I snagged two doughnuts on my way through the lobby, but this unique business opportunity was not the financial bonanza I had expected.

Such a public humiliation might have been discouraging for a guy struggling to make a living with a low-budget boating column, but it takes more than a security guard escort to shame me. But I did learn a key lesson that afternoon, a tip on prosperity my dad had tried to teach me years ago. "Nothing is free," he would say. "Certainly not your dreams."

A man is richest whose pleasures are cheapest, and I've learned to flourish in my simple flights to Fantasy Island. I call it downsizing my dream to fit market conditions, and given the lack of job security for those employed with Misfortune 500 companies, a lot of us are in the same small boat. From CAFTA to NAFTA too many of us are working for nada and falling behind in our pursuit of the American Dream. There's a ruthless spirit ravaging the ranks of the working class and he swings a mean sickle. All across corporate America, companies are eliminating positions, redistributing work overseas, and scaling back their health benefits, so a lot of us are saying, "Sea ya!"

You wouldn't think this surging wave of retirement would matter much in the land of sand and sun, but it seems too many of our displaced coworkers are washing up on the shores of Hopetown, Georgetown, and Roadtown, inflating the cost of retirement and making paupers out of the rest of us. A few years back, a friend admitted with some embarrassment that his first winter in the Abacos had cost him more than he'd planned.

"My company had just merged with another firm, and it was obvious that our division was heading for some big layoffs. For years my wife and I had been talking about going cruising but that was as far as we'd ever gone with it — just to the talking stage.

"Then one Tuesday they summoned us in for a company-wide conference call. That morning I arrived as vice president of marketing and planning development — and left unemployed and vice-poor from my dependence on fine wine and good cigars. Living on our boat in the Bahamas suddenly looked like an attractive alternative to food stamps. I had read a few books on how much we'd need for a winter of cruising, but you don't really know if those figures are accurate until you do it yourself. I was perfectly willing to trade my Honda Accord for an anchorage off Manjack Cay, but I never figured it would cramp my style so much. Now that we're cruising, I've developed a new appreciation for domestic wines. If it doesn't come in a half-gallon box with a screw-top cap, it stays on the shelf."

Well, I'm proud to say I did a little downsizing myself, trimming ten feet off my Ranger 33 in hopes of pulling within a boat's length of my dream. I was still in a state of mourning over the sale of our last sailboat when I got a letter from my editor offering me a Ranger 23 at a good price. Gary Mull always placed speed over comfort, and from my summers of Wednesday-night racing, I remembered the Ranger 23 as a quick little boat.

Our family had already defined the parameters for our next boat. It was to be slow, fat, and cheap. Bennie and the boys were tired of cracking elbows and noggins on the bulkhead, and I refused to become involved with another boat that demanded a mortgage payment for conjugal visits, so I insisted that we be boat-debt-free.

"One more thing," Bennie added, as if I might forget. "I'm not going to have another boat that does that falling-over thing. If the boat can't stand up on its own without falling over at the first sign of wind, then I say we leave it at the dock."

I found the small sloop looking neglected but stout on a trailer parked in a corner of the Lake Norman Yacht Club. The tires on the trailer were flat, a row of pine seedlings was growing along the toe rail, and a large amount of water had found its way into the cabin. So of course I bought the boat.

As is the case with many of life's small pleasures, that little sailboat invigorated our spirit of adventure and rejuvenated my dream of island hopping. I promised the boys that one day it would become their boat, and after a summer of wiring, plumbing, and drilling holes in the cabin we had it ready for the Bahamas. I had downsized the boat but not my dream. I could never do that. "Hope that is seen is no hope at all," the Apostle Paul says, because no one hopes for what he already has. Mark Twain, that other great theologian, put it this way. "Faith is believing what you know ain't so."

To continue on in the face of adversity, to get up when you've been knocked down, is not only the mark of a real man but the natural response of someone created in the image of God. To quit and give up may seem like the normal reaction to hurt and disappointment, but it is exactly the opposite response of a resilient spirit. We may knuckle under and cry out for a time, but we cannot stay down. The human spirit will not allow it. Despite the pain of our disappointments we are compelled to rise, stand, and look up and move forward. It is what we call courage, conviction, and hope. It is the stamp of our creator.

God ripens the fruit of our spirit by allowing us to experience circumstances in which we are tempted to rain down curses instead of blessings and condemnation instead of gratitude. The shortcut is to quit, but it's through testing that our character is developed. Every behavior is motivated by a belief, every action prompted by an attitude. For those of us with Christ in our heart and eternity in our future the horizon holds the promise of sunshine even when all the world is storm.

The Bahamas are not Eden and my family is not God, but both reflect a little of his glory. That's why some day I hope to take that Ranger 23 to the Bahamas. It's not how I'd hoped to reach the islands, but it's better than giving in to despair and giving up on my dreams, because let's face it — even screw-top wine taste like the finest Merlot when poured in a plastic cup at Manjack Cay.

➤ **Hard Aground hint:** "Passion is the echo of God's voice in the hallways of our soul." —DAVID JEREMIAH

➤ **Passage markers:** *For in this hope we were saved. But hope that is seen is no* *hope at all. Who hopes for what he already has?* —Romans 8:24. For further guidance read Isaiah 43:18–19.

➤ **Prayer focus:** Those who are tempted to give up on God and his plans for abundant living.

16

Boat Borrowship

IF YOU WERE TO BELIEVE THE PROPAGANDA PROMOTED AT MOST BOAT shows you might think that buying a boat would be a joyful experience. I wouldn't know myself, since I've never really "bought" a boat — at least not in the old-fashioned way of paying for something in full. Mostly I just borrow one from the bank and return it when I've run out of money and they've run out of patience.

Our family has become something of a foster home for boats that have no place to go, because it's for sure we can't go too far in the kinds of boats I keep bringing home. Boat borrowship may not be a wise investment of my time and talents, but it keeps the bank in business and my boat surveyor stocked with surf wax.

When I "borrowed" our ancient Piver trimaran a few years ago I had a short but simple set of borrowing points. The boat had to sail flat, seal tight, and sell cheaply. I had already suffered and recovered through a bad case of boat-mortgage matrimony and wasn't going to be lured into another one of those painful boat-custody relationships where I worked all week and some weekends to maintain a boat that I could visit only on holidays.

Bennie, our housemother, our budget director, and the primary sponsor of the "Earth is round, so let's sail flat" theory, was keeper of the coffee can that held our boat-borrowing money. Since Bennie was particularly bothered by the design defects found in the other borrowed boats I'd brought home

— namely that they heeled over every time the sails were set — she suggested that I look for a more stable sailing vessel.

"A condo would be nice. Do they sell condos at the boat shows?" she asked.

I said they did not, but they did sell the type of catamaran we'd been eyeing in the charter brochures. When I returned home from the show and saw the small stash of fives and twenties we'd salvaged from our last boat-borrowing disaster, however, I concluded we'd have to restrict our search to the narrow creeks and dirty boatyards where insurance companies often abandoned busted boats after hurricanes. A few weeks later, I spent the better part of a warm Saturday trying to coax Camp Don Lee fleet commander John Farmer to part with one of his busted boats. I explained to John that the one boat that seemed to show the most promise, and thus was the pick of the litter, was a sunken sloop blocking the main channel to his canoe dock.

"It's become a navigational hazard, John. All that remains above water is the bow and part of the companionway. The salon is buried under two feet of mud and the engine is submerged. The only thing that boat is good for is stabilizing the sandbar that's filling in your creek. I'd be doing you and the camp kids a favor if I hauled it away."

Despite my best efforts to denigrate the flagship of his sunken armada, John reasoned that there might yet be some value in his floundering fleet, so he pulled the boat off the market — though not off the sandbar. This form of boat hunting proved to be both frustrating and fruitless, but it wasn't long afterwards that I found another abandoned boat that matched the meager funds of our coffee can. You see, just about every time the boys and I would return from Beaufort or Ocracoke on our Ranger 23 sailboat, the boys would look longingly at the wooden trimaran docked across from us and say, "Dad, that's the boat for us."

I wasn't sure why the boys kept saying this, since the boat looked like a mud-splattered doublewide trailer that had fallen off its foundations and slipped into the creek. There weren't any opening windows or ports, and the only access into the cabin was through a submarine hatch cut through the middle of the deck. I told the boys that their mother would never go for a boat like this, since its greatest asset was a surf sticker proclaiming "Longboards Rule." Squatting beside the dock with those two beady eyes peering out across a narrow nose, she looked like a bald seagull with flesh-colored pockmarks on her scalp. I'm speaking of the boat, you understand, not Bennie.

What the vessel lacked in Catalina comforts, though, she made up for in square footage, so we "borrowed" the boat. Now I was the caretaker of a wooden trimaran that had just enough deck space to host the harbor happy hour or a small church service, and depending on the delegation and denomination we could do both at the same time. The boat's official name was *Kontigo*, but you wouldn't know that since I never painted the name on the hulls. When folks wanted to know how they'd spot us when we pulled into an anchorage, I told them that we look like the cruising Clampetts. I used a wooden yardstick as a tiller extension, steered from a Wal-Mart lounge chair positioned in the cockpit, and kept wet, dirty clothes pinned to the lifelines to discourage the gulls from unloading their arsenal on our deck. (Gulls don't have much pride, but there are some things even they won't poop on.) For a long time I had the silly notion that I would take *Kontigo* to the islands, but Bennie assured me the boat wasn't "see" worthy.

"See, you can't sit up in the bunks, you can't cook in the galley, and I'm not going to go to the bathroom in that space you call the head. If you want me to go with you to the islands on that boat — and I pray you do not — you'll have to make some structural changes to the living quarters."

So I did. I sold the boat and bought a condo.

No, seriously, I paid a fellow a large sum of money to take a chainsaw to the deck of *Kontigo*. He raised the roof, ripped up the deck, and refitted the rigging. He added two additional bunks, expanded head area, and built a full galley. When the project was completed we'd doubled the living space on *Kontigo* and tripled my boat mortgage.

Then I sold the boat.

Okay, now I'm not kidding. I really did sell the boat. I sold it for twice what I'd paid but only half of what I'd invested, because in the end, the bank had run out of patience with me. Thank goodness God isn't like that. He doesn't run out of patience with us just because we turn out to be a losing investment.

Scripture tells us that while we were still dead in our sins, he redeemed us. He wasn't looking for a bargain when he saved me. He was looking for a wretch. A derelict. A rotten boat sinking in the mud of my sins.

God doesn't call the equipped. He equips the called. He's not looking for the famous and fortunate, he's seeking the faithful. He's searching for those preoccupied with finding him, because what we allow to occupy our minds may become our occupation, and when we meditate on him daily, his work can become our vocation. It's hard to have compassion when you don't have passion — and my passion for God has allowed me to sail to some pretty neat places. In fact, it is my mission field.

The heart of the matter is serving God. What's in your heart?

➤ **Hard Aground hint:** When Jesus wanted to throw a party he didn't invite the good people. He invited the sick, the sinners, the tax collectors, and the prostitutes. If you feel like you're unworthy of a place at the feast, take heart. You're in good company — at least if you're in the company of Christ.

➤ **Passage markers:** *What is impossible with men is possible with God.* —Luke 18:27. For further guidance read I Timothy 6:17.

➤ **Prayer focus:** Those who feel that their lives are worthless and their purpose in life meaningless.

17

Give Me Your Tired, Your Poor, Your Muddled Masses of Masts

WE'RE ENTERING THE HEART OF BOAT-SELLING SEASON, AND YOU KNOW what that means. From now until corporate American decides to in-source some work back to our cities and citizens, you can go to any convention center in America and find some very desperate, former dot-com marketing types selling motor boats on straight commission. It's a pathetic sight to see men and women who just a few administrations ago were pulling in six-figure incomes reduced to misrepresenting the fuel capacity of a Bayliner. But in this new global economy, change is inevitable. Change is good. Change is all I have in my pocket.

Which is why I've come up with this novel way for acquiring my next sailboat. I call it "free." Here's how free works. You have a boat. You give it to me. You don't have a boat any more. I'm certain even China can't beat that price.

Now I know what you're thinking. You're probably saying to yourself, Why would a guy like me offer to take a boat for free and not even charge a small retainer fee for my services? Well, I'll tell you why. Because no one should take advantage of the destitute and distressed, and as we know, anyone who owns a boat is more than a little distressed.

I'm surprised that no one came up with this "free boat" deal sooner, but I've always been on the cutting edge of new ideas. Before Al Gore invented the

Internet I'd already coined the term "information highway." I didn't know what it meant at the time. I just knew it would be big. Really big. Large on a grand scale. Now my information highway is speeding relief to everyone else who's stuck with high mortgage rates or wants to meet the person of their dreams. It just shows you how far out there I am.

The concept of "free boat" seems simple enough, but you'd be surprised how many people in the marine industry get confused when I try to explain it to them. For example, last month I called the broker of a Moody 31 — that's a type of sailboat, not a Howard Dean post-primary political speech — and told him about my "free boat" deal.

Broker: "Let me get this straight. You're asking me to go back to the seller and see if he'll give you the boat?"

Eddie: "Yep, that pretty much sums up my offer."

Broker: "So you're not asking for a reduction in price?"

Eddie: "Heck no. He can keep it listed at the full price for all I care."

Broker: "But you want it for free?"

Eddie: "Exactly."

Broker: "Boy, are you nuts?"

Eddie: "Nope. Just trying to help out a fellow — Hello? Hello?"

He was on a cell phone.

By the way, the cell phone wasn't my idea. If it had been, it'd be free. In fact, I'll give you mine. It works only half the time, like when I was talking to that broker, and doesn't work at all in Oriental except under a certain tree in the village that only Wally knows about, and he's not telling me because he's basically renting out lawn chairs under the bottom branches. He knows if he told me where the hot spot was I'd expect to sit for free. I'm telling you this just so you'll understand that not everyone is as philanthropic as me.

One of the by-products of the free boat exchange program is the "boomerang effect." That one was mine too — the "boomerang effect." With the boomerang effect you give something away to get something else in return. Like, say, you're the head of a large corporation and your job is to make stuff, so you do something dumb like move all your factories to a country where they can't spell or sell your products. Well, for swapping smarts for stupid you get bankruptcy and a government bailout. This is just one example of the boomerang effect. I'm sure you can think of others.

In fact, in the Gospel of Luke, Jesus mentions my boomerang concept when he says, "Forgive, and you will be forgiven. Give, and it will be given to you. A good measure, pressed down, shaken together and running over, will be poured into your lap. For with the measure you use, it will be measured to you." I suppose if I had to rate the size of my measuring cup by that definition it would be little more than a teaspoon. It's close to blasphemy to mention Jesus and a rock star, even a great one, in the same sentence but Paul McCartney once sang, "In the end, the love you take is equal to the love you make." But both Christ and McCartney understand that it's not the taking, the grabbing, and consuming of life that defines the measure of man. It's how much he gives of himself with no expectation of reward. Giving is the grease that lubricates those relationships caught in a bind.

But that broker in South Carolina didn't see it that way, and he didn't give me the chance to explain all the benefits of my free boat program, either. Here's the main benefit to the seller: your weekends are free.

Okay, so what does that mean exactly? Well for starters, if you give me your boat you'll no longer have to spend Saturdays changing the oil in that old Yanmar engine of yours. "Yan," by the way, is Japanese for "dump it in" and "Mar," as we know, is Spanish for "sea." But you already knew this because you have a boat. The other thing you'll get for free is more money in your pocket. That's because you won't be spending money on dockage fees and boatyard bills. In fact, if you give me your boat I guarantee you'll have enough money left over at the end of the first month to buy almost a full tank of gas for a Ford Explorer.

I test marketed my free boat program last fall to see if it was a sound business plan. I contacted Norm over at Bay River Pottery. He said he had a boat. I asked if I could have it for free. He said sure. Now I have a very nice Sunfish and Norm has more time to make those little pots he's peddling in Bayboro. It doesn't take a future MBA recruit from Duke to see that making and selling more pots was a good business decision for Norm.

So the next time you're tempted to say to your broker, "But I can't reduce the price any lower — I'm already giving the darn thing away," just remember: you're a candidate for the free boat program, and I'm just the man to take your tired, your poor, your muddled masses of masts and put them to good use.

➤ **Hard Aground hint:** It is better to give than receive, so if you're struggling with an abundance of blessings give them to someone in need.

➤ **Passage markers:** *No one who has left home or wife or brothers or parents or children for the sake of the kingdom of God will fail to receive many times as much in this age and, in the age to come, eternal life.* —Luke 18:29–30. For further guidance read Luke 18:18–22.

➤ **Prayer focus:** Those weighed down with material wealth and afraid to let go, trust God, and set sail for the abundant life he promised.

18

Naming Rights

SOME TIME BACK I WENT TO GREAT PAINS TO EXPLAIN THE BENEFITS of my "free boat" program, but it seems that some of my readers — okay, all of you, completely missed the meaning of my message. Apparently you thought I was kidding. So in case you were wondering what I really meant by my free boat program, let me make it clear: I WANTED A FREE BOAT.

Don't even try to apologize now and pass along some hand-me-down yacht tied to a drooping finger pier at the end of Smith Creek. I'm not Captain Ron and this isn't some Goodwill drop box I'm running over here at Whittaker Creek.

No one except Norm at Bay River Pottery gave me a boat — and he only gave me an old Sunfish. So I went and got a sailboat the same way you probably got yours — I overstated my income and forged my wife's signature on the loan application.

Now I own a boat that is depreciating in value faster than computer programming skills in America, and because I have absolutely no idea how I'm going to make the payments on this boat, I have concocted a new financing programming that I like to call "sponsorship."

I stole that idea from NASCAR.

You remember NASCAR, don't you? That's the National Association of Stock Car Automobile Racing that used to race Plymouths, Buicks, Chevys, and Fords at places like Rockingham and North Wilkesboro. In North Carolina

NASCAR was once as popular as cigarettes and corn liquor, but about the time pig farming replaced tobacco as the state's cash crop, NASCAR moved the racing to Kansas, Chicago, and California where "running good" is something you do in sneakers, not in the Snickers–M&M's–Crunch Bar car driven by Ken Schrader.

Anyway, I've decided to do like NASCAR — sell out — and pay for my new purchase by offering the naming rights to my boat. This is also a very popular practice for sporting facilities. I know this because the Charlotte racetrack is now called the Lowe's Motor Speedway, even though they don't carry lumber or plumbing fixtures at the racetrack. Selling the naming rights is also a very popular way of funding public radio where, it seems, every news program is underwritten by the family of Robert Wood Johnson.

I tried to contact the family of Mr. Johnson to see if they wanted to buy the naming rights to my boat, but when I got hold of the Wood Brothers Racing Team, Chip Wood said he'd never heard of Robert Wood Johnson and was pretty sure the Wood brothers never had a brother named Robert.

"We had a cousin Bobby who died some years ago, but he never worked much and I knowed he weren't the kind to listen to public radio. Heck, he couldn'ta even *spelt* radio. He's the only dead Wood I know of. You might want to check with Junior Johnson, though. Sounds like some of his kin."

Junior Johnson doesn't actually answer his own phone, did you know that? I left a message, but while I'm waiting for Junior to return my call, I thought I'd give some of the businesses in Oriental the chance to sponsor my boat. For a small donation of, say, whatever you can send, I'll paint the name of your daddy or business on the side of my new-old Bristol 29.9.

If this works as planned — and almost nothing I ever do does so this probably will — you're likely to hear something like this the next time I run aground:

"Well, ladies and gentlemen, it looks like the Toucan Grill–Paddle Pamlico–TownDock Bristol 29.9 sponsored in part today by Sail Loft Realty has run out of the channel again. It looked like she was coming out of that dog-leg turn three just beyond marker two when the M & M's keel scraped the shoal just west of the Whittaker Creek channel and planted the Maxwell

House–Good-to-the-last-drop–at-The-Bean bow on that thumb of sand. The crew looks to be pulling the Cape Lookout Yacht Charters sail cover back on now. Is that how you saw it, B. P.?"

"Huh?"

"I asked if that's the way you saw it."

"Saw what?"

"That boat run aground."

"Oh, sorry, about that, D. W. I was practicing my lines for the next NASCAR video game."

"Which one?"

"'He can't be happy about that, Bob.'"

"No, not which line. I meant, which version of the game?"

"Does it matter?"

"No, not really. So did you see the boat run aground or not?"

"Oh yeah, I saw it brush the shoal up in turn three. I think the Triton's Cove–Deaton's depth sounder blowed a fuse. It's a real shame, too. That boat had a chance to do well today."

In this life I had a real chance to do well too, but I ran aground and when I did, I gathered a new name. Loser. The last book of the Bible assures me I'll get a new name if I overcome. I'm not sure what that means, but I'm looking forward to a new name. I'm not so keen on the one I have now. "Eddie" is always portrayed as a dimwit ne'er-do-well, which in my case is an accurate description, but I hate the name anyway. To give you some idea of just how bad a name it is, during the closing days of World War II Eddie Slovik became the first U.S. soldier to be executed for desertion since the Civil War. During the 1988 Winter Olympics Eddie "the Eagle" Edwards, with his Coke-bottle glasses and "Mr. Magoo" persona, set a new low for ski jumping by finishing dead last. Eddie Haskell was always getting Beaver in trouble and Eddie Munster was, well, just weird.

So yes, I'm hoping God will have a new name for me in his kingdom. One that means winner, not loser. One that carries the royalty of a king, not a peasant. One that reflects the glory of my Father, not the failures of my life. For those kind of naming rights I'd give my soul.

➤ **Hard Aground hint:** "Run" is a right fine word for almost any sentence in NASCAR. For example, "We run good" is something you want to happen in a race but "They run us down" is not. "We run over some oil on the track, got into the wall, and tore up a good car" will excuse almost any wreck — unless you're Tony Stewart, in which case it was just another bonehead move.

➤ **Passage markers:** *He who has an ear, let him hear what the Spirit says to the churches. To him who overcomes, I will give some of the hidden manna. I will also give him a white stone with a new name written on it, known only to him who receives it.* —Revelation 2:17. For further guidance read John 15:11–17.

➤ **Prayer focus:** Those who want to change their name from "loser" to "victor," from slave of sin to child of God.

19

Not a Yacht Happening
in My Slip

I SOLD OUR 1967 PIVER 30 TRIMARAN RECENTLY, SO THERE'S NOT A YACHT happening in my slip these days. I asked my wife what features she would like to have in our next boat. Bennie grimaced the way she does when she gets a touch of gas, then walked down the dock to take the boys wakeboarding on her dad's motorboat. That should have been my hint that she has grown tired of the kinds of boats I keep bringing home, but nobody's ever accused me of being the freshest fry in the Happy Meal.

Bennie wasn't tracking my movements too closely when I purchased that old Piver 30. By the time she got around to saying "No, we don't need another sailboat — certainly not an old wooden trimaran that looks like a double-wide trailer on water skis," I had the boat sitting on the mud in my slip. It was a reckless move that strained our relationship, but I got to keep the boat, and I learned in church years ago that it is easier to receive forgiveness than permission. Actually I learned this lesson playing church softball, but I still consider it sound theological doctrine.

Anyway, Bennie is a little fussy when it comes to my brand of boating. Her idea of the perfect passage begins when the anchor is set, the bimini's deployed, and a nest of cushions has been configured in a corner of the cockpit. When the boys and I have fled in the dinghy to some remote stretch of distant shoreline, Bennie melts into the cockpit and naps in the shade of the dodger.

To her this is the essence of cruising. During these quiet moments of pink sun-
sets and salt-laden sea breezes, she will reluctantly admit that she enjoys this
type of boating. It's the sailing part that turns her stomach.

If sailboats are built to heel then Bennie is bound to squeal. During our
last passage to Ocracoke I was down below fixing lunch while Bennie lay in the
cockpit with a cold dishrag draped across her forehead. Every few minutes I'd
poke my head into the cockpit to make sure the autopilot was still automatically taking us off course, and to see if Bennie had fallen over or jumped in.
During one of these inspections, I brought her lunch on a plastic plate and
asked, "Do you want to eat this sandwich yourself, or should I just throw it over
the side and save you the trouble?" She glared at me the way she does when I
ask about that other activity wives sometimes find a bother. I decided to keep
my mouth shut the rest of the passage. I felt fortunate that one of us could.

When the boys and I go cruising we feast on Pop-Tarts and hot dogs and
if it were left to me, we'd eat spaghetti every night. Bennie tolerates this aquatic
camping lifestyle because she knows this is my passion, but she's made it clear
that she's ready for a boat that keeps her warm in the winter, cool in the summer, and dry year round. She wants a boat with a two-burner stove in the gal-

ley and enough counter space to drain the pots, plates, and bowls. She wants a boat with a refrigeration unit that stays cold longer than a day, and enough storage space to hold a week's worth of provisions. She wants a V-berth with more "U" than "V" in the berthing canal and a head equipped with a toilet that doesn't have to be pumped like a car jack. What she wants, in other words, is a different husband. And a yacht.

I told her that by definition a "yacht" was any boat we couldn't afford, and since we've never been able to afford any of the boats I've owned, that she's already sailed on a number of fine yachts. She said my definition was flawed.

"If you insist on buying another sailboat," she said, "and I pray you do not, but if you do, then at least get a quality yacht and not some old worn-out boat like you did last time."

"I thought our last boat was the perfect yacht."

"You thought that old wooden trimaran was a yacht? Get a clue, Eddie! If the listing broker is an insurance adjuster working from an RV at a busted-boat auction, then it's not a yacht yet. If bathing on the swim platform involves standing on the stern with a sun shower slapping you in the ear, then it's not a yacht yet. If paper towels double as dishes, and plastic wine glasses would make a nice addition to the galley, then it's not a yacht yet. If going to the head involves grasping a backstay for balance, then it's not a yacht yet. If the freshest item in the icebox is a six-pack of beer, then it's not a yacht yet. If the only item in the icebox is a six-pack of beer, then it's not a yacht yet. If the icebox is really just a Styrofoam cooler you found in the parking lot of the Charlotte Motor Speedway, then it's not a yacht yet. And if our bank agrees to lend you the money, then it is absolutely not a yacht yet."

Sometimes I think my wife lacks the vision to see the potential in the discarded derelicts I keep bringing home — but then I remember she married me despite her parents' concerns that I was a work in progress. Actually, I think they said I was a piece of work. Or maybe I should get to work. In any case, it doesn't matter now because I'm too busy sailing and surfing to work.

Sometimes I lack the vision to see the potential in the people God brings into my life too. At times like this God gives me a smack upside the head to remind me that Christ died for me precisely because I was broken, battered, and beaten down. He saw what I could become, not what I was. He took a chance on me when I had no chance at all of becoming anything other than a sorry sinner and a right poor sailor.

The great tragedy of life is that we give up on people too quickly. We quit a marriage, wash our hands of a rebellious child, or abandon a friend who's imprisoned by a habit or vice that's killing them from the inside out. We pass judgment on the faults of others because we know what's right and wrong and forget how wrong we were in the sight of God before we accepted his son as our savior.

Jesus warned that we should be fast to forgive and slow to judge. "If you forgive men when they sin against you, your heavenly Father will also forgive you. But if you do not forgive men their sins, your Father will not forgive your sins." That's a damning statement. And it leaves very little wiggle room. I'm a simple man with a simple boat, and I come at life with a simple understanding of the complexities of the universe — but even I understand that comparing myself to others is a right stupid thing to do.

We are all a work in progress, all vessels in need of repair. If God hasn't given up on you yet, then neither should I. And I hope you won't give up on me either.

➤ **Hard Aground hint:** "You get tired and disgusted with me, when I can't be just what you want me to be. I still love you and I try real hard. I swear, one day, you'll have a brand new car. I even asked the Lord to try to help me: He looked down from heaven, said to tell you please; Just be patient, I'm a work in progress." —ALAN JACKSON

➤ **Passage markers:** *Forgive us our debts, as we also have forgiven our debtors.* —Matthew 6:12. For further guidance read Matthew 18:21–35.

➤ **Prayer focus:** Those who need to forgive and restore a broken relationship.

"Drop the sails," I shouted to everyone in the anchorage. This sent my crew of ten-year-old boys into action, and they immediately began stumbling over the forward hatch, tugging at their underwear and picking their noses in wonder at what I meant by this command. "The sails, dagnab it! Release the halyards and drop the sails," I shouted. "I can't turn the boat and I think we're about to run aground."

"We're already aground," Mason announced, releasing the topping lift and dropping the boom onto my head.

Part IV

Bringing the Bow to Port: Finding Your Way Back Home

20

I Got the Turkey Trots

I GOT THE TURKEY TROTS. YOU MAY HAVE A TOUCH OF THE TURKEY TROTS too if you own a boat that's shackled to a dock piling this Thanksgiving, and your friends have already crossed over. By this I mean they've already cleared the state line in Florida and are heading to the islands for the winter. But there is a cure for the turkey trots.

Turkeys, as you know from your high school World History class, are not an ethnic people living on the shores of the Black Sea. They do not share a border with Iraq and Syria. Those people are called Turks. There is also a segment of that population called the Kurds, but this is way more information than you need to know for curing the turkey trots. Just trust me when I tell you that you don't want to mention turkeys and Kurds at Thanksgiving dinner when you are passing the giblet dressing. It's not a direction you want to steer the conversation.

If you're watching TV on Thanksgiving morning you'll see some turkeys marching and strutting through the streets of New York, but that's a different kind of turkey trot. The Lord knows better than me why these turkeys would be up so early on a holiday morning, wandering through the streets of Manhattan, but I think they are confused by this "early bird gets the worm" advice. For all you turkeys let me just say, there are no worms for the early bird. There never were any worms. It was all part of a mass conspiracy to get the birds up and out so someone could steal the nest eggs of otherwise industrious turkeys. Worthless pension plans, dot-com stock options, and failed savings-and-loan holdings are but a few of the nest eggs that have gone missing. If you are a lazy turkey like me, then you would do well to sleep in and cook your own nest of eggs on Thanksgiving morning.

I caught my turkey trots a few weeks prior to Thanksgiving while anchored in Oriental harbor. I was reading my devotion and sipping coffee when the skipper of a sailboat motored past on his way by the jetty. He was alone, working the tiller and adjusting the throttle of his 27-foot sailboat. His long gray ponytail and Canadian flag testified to the fact that he'd traveled many miles already and had many more to go. As he passed, I was fully aware that by the end of November that snowbird would be someplace warm and sunny. That's when I got the turkey trots. I wanted to be flying south with him.

Turkeys don't fly. They stroll or trot, but they don't do either very fast. The sight of that Canadian snowbird flying south had focused my thoughts on what I was, and where I wasn't, instead of who I am and where I've been. That form of self-reflection can be lethal. Evaluating the state of my condition can be helpful when I'm trying to gauge how far I've come, but not when it involves comparing myself to others. When I compare my circumstances to those around me I become either conceited or discouraged but seldom grateful. Praise and anxiety are two opposing forces. So I reached for the cure and found it written in the margins of my devotional journal. Here was my first dosage. It was an entry I found from our second day of vacation that summer.

"Dinghied in and walked to the hardware store before sunrise. Bennie wants to cook noodles on the boat for dinner and we're out of denatured alcohol for the stove. It rained hard last night and they say more is coming with the tropical storm. The large ruts at the edge of the gravel driveways were full of water and it had spilled over into the bicycle lane. In some places standing water was halfway out to the double yellow line. I had to keep waiting for traffic to pass before I could walk around the puddles. It reminded me of the road beside the Conch Inn in Marsh Harbor after a shower. The air feels wet and tacky this morning, like it does in the islands. The dirt lanes of Ocracoke are rinsed clean and washed free of the ferry's regurgitated meal of mainland motorists. God, I love this place."

Here's another entry.

"Anchored on the backside of Shackleford Banks up close to the beach. The surf was huge this afternoon with the passing of Hurricane Jeanne south of us. Steep drops with fast barrels were spitting spray up the faces. There's nothing better than jumping off the stern of your boat, paddling ashore and walking through a stand of trees as a herd of horses grazes at your side. I reached the top of the sand dunes and found corduroy lines stretching back to Beaufort Channel as far as the eye could see. I suppose heaven might be like this."

I found other entries written in my prayer journal. Moments of solitude at Cape Lookout on a surprisingly warm and calm March afternoon. A starlit night on South River. An impromptu lunch with my sister and her girls on Broad Creek. But I had to stop reading. The high whine of an outboard in distress interrupted my thoughts. I stood and turned, looking over the lip of my dodger. My Canadian snowbird had missed the turn to the channel and run aground on the shoal at the edge of the Pecan Grove channel.

I thanked God that it was he who was aground and not me, and reflected on life's small blessings. Being afloat on my old boat is one kind of blessing. Finding the time and passion to enjoy the Carolina coast is another. Having the good sense to want what I already have and be grateful for what I've received is, perhaps, the best blessing of all.

For me it's the perfect cure for the turkey trots.

➤ **Hard Aground hint:** Thanksgiving is the cure for stress. Peace comes when we find we're too blessed to be stressed.

➤ **Passage markers:** *Do not be anxious about anything, but in everything, by prayer and petition, with thanksgiving, present your requests to God. And the peace of God, which transcends all understanding, will guard your hearts and your minds in Christ Jesus.* —Philippians 4:6–7. For further inspiration read Luke 6:38.

➤ **Prayer focus:** Those anxious about things other than God's will.

21

Seeds of Greed

I GUESS YOU COULD CALL ME GREEDY, BECAUSE NO MATTER HOW MUCH I have, it's never enough, at least not when it comes to cruising. Most days I sail out of Oriental, North Carolina, and depending on the direction and vigor of the wind, the depth of my slip can vary from a few inches to a few feet. The summer southwesterlies blow the water out and the nor'easters blow it in, so when it's blowing a stink out of the north and nobody wants to go sailing — well, on those days I can float my boat and go cruising. On the days when it's blowing steady out of the southwest, providing a nice reach across the Pamlico Sound, I'm hard aground and can't go anywhere except to the pool.

I tell you this because when I do escape the mud in my slip and go cruising, I leave with a different perspective than most. I'm not frustrated when I snag a shoal, since stuck is stuck no matter where I am, and since I'm usually glued to the bottom of my slip, running aground someplace new is kind of fun. Like a boating inmate confined to solitary "dock-down," when I'm offered the opportunity to explore the grounds of the penitentiary, gray skies and whitecaps look pretty good.

Now you might think that I would be content with sailing in the 99 percent of the lower Neuse River that can accommodate my shoal-draft sailboat, but I am not. I want more. I want the oceans I've never seen and the harbors I've only dreamed of. I want to nap beneath the agitated chafing of palm fronds as trees rustle in the wake of a tropical breeze. I long to explore lush hillsides steeped in foliage framed by Chardonnay streams of cascading waterfalls. In short, I want the world and all that's good in God's creation.

That's why I'm always pushing the limits of my migratory margins, venturing beyond the PVC pipes and Styrofoam floats that mark the shoals of my domain. I suffer from carnivorous cruising, and so my bending of the rules — my sailing beyond the established boundaries — is just another version of the exotic exploration that you read about in the big cruising magazines.

There was a time a few years ago when I'd get postcards from Dave and Jaja Martin as they were coming and going from Iceland or Finland or Mars. The Martins were *Cruising World*'s 1995 Seamanship Medal winners, and at the time I thought Dave was about the nuttiest guy in the galaxy, sailing to the edges of the planet like he did. I could never understand what would make someone want to sail that far from Oriental unless it was a bad set of tax laws or maybe in-laws, so before he left the last time I asked him why they were off to the North Pole.

"We want to go someplace cold," Dave replied. "I'm tired of the crowds and the bugs and the heat of the tropics. We're going someplace extreme, but not too extreme."

This from a guy who started off on a solo circumnavigation in a twenty-five foot sailboat and came home with a wife and two toddlers all packed in the same small vessel. I'll reserve judgment on Dave's definition of extreme, but I would suggest that, as with most things in life and luffing, it's all a matter of degrees.

The difference between Dave and me is that I like my degrees high on the Fahrenheit scale and low on the latitude chart. Of course, my family is quick to remind me that there's another difference that separates a pioneer like Dave Martin from myself. Dave sets off prepared for the rigors of long-distance cruising. I start off with Pop-Tarts, a wide smile, and not much more. Which is how I came to run out of water on South River this summer.

The humiliating end to another fine afternoon of sailing began as we pushed our boat out of its slip in Whittaker Creek. My buddy Pat Patterson hates to lose almost as much as I love to win, so when he hoisted the sails on his 20-foot day sailor and raced off towards South River, I felt obliged to trim the sheets of my own sailboat and run him down. I had the boys with me, but since we weren't handicapping our unofficial regatta, it was merely Pat's misfortune that he had to race single-handed. As we neared the far side of the Neuse, I got a good run on him and was about to nudge a fender under his bumper when he suddenly let the sails luff. This allowed me to take the lead, but I realized too late why he had allowed me to pass. He was expecting me to find the bottom so he wouldn't have to.

For the next few minutes it looked as though his strategy would fail. I managed to avoid most of the shoals along the channel and caught a nice lift in front of the pirate graveyard. I was certain victory was mine, so I decided to push the boundaries of South River's skinny waters and sail along the north shore. When I was sure I could clear the stern of the committee boat — which was just an old Hunter anchored off the point — I pulled the tiller over and attempted to come about. I say "attempted to come about" because the helm was firmly planted in the "forward" position and in no danger of turning left or right.

"Drop the sails," I shouted to everyone in the anchorage. This sent my crew of ten-year-old boys into action, and they immediately began stumbling over the forward hatch, tugging at their underwear and picking their noses in wonder at what I meant by this command. "The sails, dagnab it! Release the halyards and drop the sails," I shouted. "I can't turn the boat and I think we're about to run aground."

"We're already aground," Mason announced, releasing the topping lift and dropping the boom onto my head. "And I have to go to the bathroom."

I pushed the boom off my shoulder and looked over the stern to see that, sure enough, we were stuck.

"Then I guess we can take our time furling the sails," I said, handing my crew the sail ties. "I'll jump in and try to remove this crab pot from the rudder."

I knew from previous mishaps that a stiff tiller and reluctant rudder were usually an indication that a vagrant crab pot had attached itself to my boat. Since the water beneath *Kontigo* was only knee deep, I stepped into the water, yanked the crab trap free, and ordered the boys to jump in. This allowed my

son to take care of the other thing he needed to do, and then the three of us put our shoulders into the work and soon had the boat drifting towards deeper water. It was as splendid a grounding as any I've enjoyed, and it only cost me a victory in a race that didn't matter to anyone except Pat, and he tends to think too highly of his sailing abilities anyway. Others might be embarrassed at such a debacle, but I jettisoned all navigational pride long ago. Now I merely look at these astounding groundings as evidence that I'll never be ready for the rigors of global exploration. But who is? Who is really prepared for all that life can throw at us?

Rather than risk the rewards of the unknown, too many folks seek the security of sturdy walls in a dull profession. They find comfort in common surroundings and remain stuck in a port that pollutes their soul with the stagnant waste of passing days. But man was not made for confinement. He was made for adventure.

For those of us who love to sail, God has placed the call of paradise in our heart. It draws us from the satisfaction of where we are towards the possibility of what we might become. When we stop for too long, we grow stale, rot, and gather barnacles. God knows we have a tendency to sit too long, so he's always prodding us to get up and get going.

Each of us hears the call of paradise in different ways. It's that dream in your heart that you try to ignore. It's the passion that you bury for the safety of a steady paycheck. It's a hobby that's not quite a job but not quite a passing fancy either. It's a talent and a love that others confirm when they see your finished work. We hear the call and bend our ears but refuse to walk towards its sound because of the fear of failure, scorn, or poverty.

If you have heard the call, then set sail. You may run aground in the skinny waters of life, but if you keep your eyes fixed on your dreams, you'll get your boat moving forward again. Wherever you're going, that's where you'll be, so set a course for your dreams today.

➤ **Hard Aground hint:** A journey of a thousand miles begins with a cash advance at the ATM machine. —OVERHEARD ON THE PORCH AT THE BEAN IN ORIENTAL, NORTH CAROLINA

➤ **Passage markers:** *Those living far away fear your wonders; where morning dawns and evening fades you call forth songs of joy.* —Psalm 65:8. For further inspiration read John 2:110.

➤ **Prayer focus:** Those blessed with the gifts of spontaneity and carelessness.

22

Santa Pause

DEAR SANTA: I GOT ANOTHER BOAT SO YOU CAN SCRATCH THAT ONE OFF my list. I know I was pretty mad in my last letter when I complained that you had forgotten me but, my mother-in-law says you were alive and working from a plywood booth in Kinston when she was a little girl, so I think maybe you're getting old and forgetting stuff. She does that a lot too. How far back do you go?

My cousin Gina said if I talked to you to say thanks for the baby brother you brought her last year, but what she really wanted was a puppy. She said she'd never asked you for anything else before. That you could look it up if you didn't believe her. I think that's why she's not writing to you this year. You kind of got it wrong and now she doesn't believe in you as much as I do.

By the way, is there any way you can put another holiday between Christmas and Easter? There's nothing good in there now except Presidents' Day. My dad said the last president wasn't any good, and Mom thinks this one is even worse. Maybe you could do away with Presidents' Day and just give us more snow days. Right now we don't get snow except on Saturdays, and on Monday we still have to go to work and school. What's up with that?

I know you keep up with who's been bad and good, but Mom says you love everybody. I think that would be hard to do. There are only four people in our family and I don't like any of them sometimes. By the way, is it true my

friend Pat won't get any gifts if he uses his sailing words in the house? I'm just asking because he doesn't believe in you, and I think that's why you didn't bring him a new sailboat last year. I know you have to believe to get gifts, and I do, but I didn't get a new sailboat last year either. Sometimes I use my sailing words in the house, too. I'd try harder if I knew for certain you were real.

Do you have trouble coming into America from Canada? Grandma says she gets searched every time she comes back with her heart medicine. Do you have to take off your boots and belt too? I think it's good that we're keeping mean people out, but not if it stops you from visiting.

I really like the Christmas lights we have these days. They're better than the old ones I see in pictures. And there's a lot more of them, too. Grandma says when she was a girl they only put lights on the trees, not on the whole house. She says it looks like the Griswolds have moved into our neighborhood, but I know everybody on our creek and I haven't met a Griswold yet. Sometimes Grandma doesn't take her medication and gets confused.

But we could use some better music. I hope this doesn't hurt your feelings, but no one sings like that any more. Can you write some new songs? I heard Jimmy Buffett singing "Jingle Bells" on the radio the other day, but it wasn't any better than the old version. I don't think he's the right guy for the job.

Why do old people smell funny? Just wondering.

Mom says I should spend more time praying to God and less time worrying about whether I've been good or bad. She says that God doesn't care if I've been good or bad, only if I trust my life to his son. I don't know what she means by this. Can you help me understand? I can't believe God gives bad people good stuff and good people bad stuff. That doesn't seem fair, but Mom says he's a just God and we don't see everything that goes on. I just wish he had a booth at the mall, like you, so I could ask him these things.

Speaking of asking for stuff, here are some things I want.

Can you make August colder? Sometimes when I go to Cape Lookout it's so hot I have to sleep with my feet in the ice cooler.

Can you put more water in our slip? Last year my boat was stuck a lot because all the water went away. If you're sending it to another part of the world, can I have it back?

Can you help Ben Casey sell more books? I like the pictures he takes. Maybe you could leave a few of his books on the coffee table of every home you visit. I think that would make a nice Christmas present.

Can you find the screw to my eyeglasses? I dropped it in the parking lot of The Bean, and now I have to use duct tape to keep my glasses together.

Can you make corn crab chowder soup a regular item on the menu at M & M's? Sometimes when I go, they're out, and I have to eat a salad.

Finally, can you keep Oriental like it is? I don't want it to grow up like I have to. Getting older and bigger stinks.

Your friend,

Eddie Jones

P.S. If you want to bring me a sailboat bigger than a Sunfish, I won't send it back. Or maybe you could bring Pat one. That might help him believe in you more.

➤ **Hard Aground hint:** In the old days, it was not called the Holiday season; the Christians called it Christmas and went to church; the Jews called it Hanukkah and went to synagogue; the atheists went to parties and drank. People passing each other on the street would say "Merry Christmas" or "Happy Hanukkah" or (to the atheists) "Look out for the wall!" —DAVE BARRY

➤ **Passage markers:** *You want something but don't get it. You kill and covet, but you cannot have what you want. You quarrel and fight. You do not have, because you do not ask God. When you ask, you do not receive, because you ask with wrong motives, that you may spend what you get on your pleasures.* —James 4:2–3. For further inspiration read John 14:1–14.

➤ **Prayer focus:** Those seeking to discern the difference between their needs and desires and God's purpose in withholding both for a season.

23

Recovering from a Sinking Spell

I WASN'T THERE THE DAY TOM'S BOAT SANK, BUT THE WAY I HEARD THE STORY — and it's possible I didn't hear it correctly since I tend to lose focus and facts when I've been sailing the Sunfish — was that Tom brought this old wooden motor boat down from New Jersey and drowned it in the slip behind his house on Lake Norman.

Tom loves boats. When he was our neighbor on the lake he kept two motorboats and a Jet Ski tied behind his house, one of which was always in a state of disrepair. It's a tribute to Tom's good sense that he rode the Jet Ski more than he drove the motorboats because as any one who has ever ridden a Jet Ski knows, they're faster and funner than a broken-down motorboat. Jet Skis are loud and annoying the way a yipping dog is — unless the yipping dog happens to be your dog. I hate a Jet Ski when it's under the bottom of some teenage boy pumped up on testosterone, but I think one looks just fine under my rump. Tom's Jet Ski was fast. This is especially important on Lake Norman when summer thunderstorms roll in quickly and the next cold drink is back at the dock. That's how I came to meet Tom and hear about his dunked motorboat. I was fishing in his cooler for refreshment.

Tom and Cathy moved into the neighborhood a few weeks before Memorial Day to assume the mortgage on a split-level ranch on our cul-de-sac. This provided my father-in-law with a neighbor who disliked goose droppings and boat wake almost as much as he did. The afternoon our family arrived to begin the summer sailing season Tom invited us over to their dock for drinks. Now here is where the story gets a little fuzzy, mostly because I was into one of Tom's fruity rum drinks when he began telling the tale.

Tom explained that in early May he had decided to truck his old wooden motorboat down from New Jersey so he could use it on the lake. As will often happen with old wooden boats, when she tried to go swimming, she drowned. Fortunately for Tom, however, the boat was still in the slings at the boatyard.

Tom said all wooden boats sink when they are re-baptized, and that people with wooden boats accept this behavior the way cat owners accept hair on the couch. Tom went on to explain how he had been suffering from separation depression since moving to the lake. Separation depression is an ailment that afflicts a boat owner who's been estranged from his boat. What Tom didn't know, though, was that his boat was suffering from separation depression, too — just in a different way. The wooden planks were peeling away from the ribs of the frame.

Dropping the boat back into the water had cured Tom of his separation depression, but old wooden boats are not as easily healed. Unlike fine wine, they do not mellow with the passing of years. They turn rancid and rot, is what they do.

Tom's Toucan appeared to be adjusting fine to the fresh lake water. The wooden planks expanded nicely, closing the gaps in the hull. When she seemed to be floating on her own, Tom fired her up, slipped the dock lines, and motored across the lake and into the cove at the end of Bayshore Drive. That first month after Tom and his boat were together again, he would stroll down the dock, pull up a deck chair, and hook a tanned ankle over the railing. He would gaze south across the narrow waters of our cove and above the pine tops towards Charlotte, where he would smile smugly to himself as he thought of his poor neighbors inching their way home along on I-77, because he already was . . . home, I mean.

Then towards the end of that second week, while Tom was away on business, his precious Toucan sank to the bottom of the lake. The insurance adjuster guessed that the boat had opened a seam somewhere below the water line. But, as I said, that was just a guess. The truth was no one knew for certain why the boat sank. It just did.

Life is like that sometimes, dragging us down for no good reason, drowning our dreams under waves of disappointment. Washing away our wishes with tears. Wherever there is tragedy you can be sure God is nearby. That's where his love burns brightest.

We rarely see God's purpose in our pain and failures. We are not promised protection from the wind and floods that swamp our boat and dreams — only peace amid the storm. The Apostle Paul says in Philippians that "the peace of God, which passes all understanding, will guard your hearts and minds in Christ Jesus." The Greek word for "peace" here means to "bind together" something that has been broken or disjointed, patching it back together. When our dreams are shattered, they are scattered like so many shards of glass, but God can put the pieces back together — oftentimes in ways we would never have imagined. Our shattered dreams become the stained-glass window of our soul. Tom's boat sank out back of his house that afternoon, but his dreams didn't.

He settled with the insurance company and moved on. In fact, he moved to Oriental. That's what he was coming to tell me that weekend at their lake house. He and Cathy were leaving Lake Norman to open a restaurant near my marina. Tom and Cathy have "sunk" just about everything they have into making this new Toucan float. Tom probably wouldn't want me to tell you how excited he is to be in Oriental, but I'll tell you anyway. He's excited. Mighty excited.

And I'm excited too. I've missed those "dock tales" we used to share out back of his lake house. I've missed riding on his Jet Ski. I've even missed that crazy killer cat of his. But mostly I've missed those fruity rum drinks he made and the slow days we spent on his dock pondering what we'd do if our ship came in. Tom's new ship is called the Toucan Grill and it's docked along the harbor in Oriental. And I, for one, am glad it is.

➤ **Hard Aground hint:** Every valley has two mountains, so avoid looking back at your disappointments and look up instead, because that's where you'll find the next mountaintop experience." —UNKNOWN

➤ **Passage markers:** *And we know that in all things God works for the good of those who love him, who have been called according to his purpose.* —Romans 8:28. For further inspiration read Acts 27:1–44.

➤ **Prayer focus:** Those blessed with adversity and struggling to reach the next mountaintop experience.

24

Another Year Has Croaked

AFTER 364 GRUELING DAYS, WE ARE DOWN TO THE LAST MOMENTS OF the year 2003, and you know what that means. We're nearing the final days of Clay Aiken's reign as America's most fabricated idol. Based on the most recent measurement of goods and services produced by our country, Aiken was the only product one hundred percent manufactured in America last year. Everything else, including California's new governor and the SARS virus, was imported from another country.

This is the time of the season when we pass judgment on the good and bad moments of the year and, if we're really honest, secretly hope that next year every adolescent boy in America will learn to pull their pants up. Because I'm committed to keeping the spirit of the New Year flowing until the last of the spirits have been poured, I've compiled a list of the best and worst moments.

THE BEST — The TownDock webcam during Hurricane Isabel. Watching the water rise over Hodges Street and the top steps of The Bean without having to actually stand in the wind and rain was the best part of the storm.

THE WORST — Hurricane Isabel. Please . . . can't we order one of these storms for Myrtle Beach? I'm certain they deserve it more than we do.

THE BEST — The new inlet just north of Hatteras Village. Hurricane Isabel created a new island, an exclusive enclave for those seeking the quiet and solitude of island living. Anytime a remote island is created at the edge of civilization it's a good thing.

THE WORST — Dumping $1.4 million worth of sand into the new inlet and proving, once again, that as long as man and the government have more money than sense we will squander whatever blessings we receive.

THE BEST — Selling my 1968 Piver trimaran to Wym and Gail. It truly was one of the happiest days of my life.

THE WORST — Selling my boat for half of what I had in it and spending the rest of the year boatless and adrift while I paid off the balance of the boat mortgage.

THE BEST — Spending every available moment sailing Pat's 20-foot Cygnus day sailor around the Neuse River. Even a friend's small, tired old boat is better than no boat at all.

THE WORST — Sailing Pat's cramped day sailor among a fleet of newer, nicer yachts and wishing we had someplace to sleep other than under the stars and frost.

THE BEST — Corn crab chowder soup at M & M's after a night sail to the dinghy dock.

THE WORST — Walking up the street from the dinghy dock only to discover that M & M's was out of Corn crab chowder soup.

THE BEST — Holding my first book signing at The Bean in early May and selling almost all the books I brought.

THE WORST — Standing in front of The Bean in May, wearing a pair of sandals and shorts as a nor'easter swept down the Pamlico Sound and wishing I were wearing my snowboarding outfit.

THE BEST — Having Dave Martin, Elaine Marshall, and my former Bible Study Fellowship leader stop by to get an autographed copy of my book.

THE WORST — Not having everyone else in North Carolina stop in to buy my book.

THE BEST — Getting a free Sunfish from Norm and Candace at Bay River Pottery.

THE WORST — Not having enough time left in the season to repair my new boat before the first hard freeze.

THE BEST — Spending New Year's Eve in Oriental and helping drop the Croaker from atop *HeatherBell*'s mast.

THE WORST — Spending New Year's Eve in Oriental without my wife, Bennie, and having no one to share a Croaker kiss with.

THE BEST — Any day in Oriental.

THE WORST — All the other days.

Here's to last year and hoping we get more of the good and less of the bad.

➤ **Hard Aground hint:** When it comes to making New Year's resolutions, as I said last year, I never repeat myself.

➤ **Passage markers:** *There is a time for everything, and a season for every activity under heaven: a time to be born and a time to die, a time to plant and a time to uproot, a time to kill and a time to heal, a time to tear down and a time to build, a time to weep and a time to laugh, a time to mourn and a time to dance, a time to scatter stones and a time to gather them.* —Ecclesiastes 3:1–5. For further inspiration read Isaiah 40:29–31.

➤ **Prayer focus:** Those who know it's time to step out in faith but keep hitting the snooze button.

25

Bringing the Bow to Port

THE GUY WHO'S BEEN SUPERINTENDENT, ARCHITECT, AND PRIMARY NAIL driver on my boat-building project walked off the job this week, leaving me with a half-baked boat and a fully blown budget. To be accurate, he rode off on his bicycle and is hiding in a single-wide trailer. The impact of his work stoppage remains the same, though. My 1968 Piver 30 trimaran, which was already a work of art before we began this multihull renovation, is now a real masterpiece — listing a little more to the abstract than the classical side of art. The sad part is that I still don't have the name of the boat painted on the hulls.

The boat's official name is *Kontigo*, but you wouldn't know that, since I've never painted the name on the hulls. Painting the words along the outer amas isn't going to make her sail any faster, point up any further, or pass a Coast Guard inspection any sooner, but it will help cover over the areas where the Sears Weatherbeater has chipped off. It might also force me to give her a permanent P. O. box.

I've been reluctant to, ah, *address* this issue these past few years, since I was never sure when the bank was going to call and ask me to return their boat. I've seen the way other "yacht" owners use the term "home port" to describe their boat's home address, and it makes me think that I missed something in that one Power Squadron course I audited fifteen years ago. When I see the gold-gilded words Fort Collins, CO, painted beside the swim ladder of a hulking Hatteras tied to a fuel dock, I know the skipper isn't sailing the boat back to

114

Colorado. His house, family, and place of vocation may be in the Rockies, but that's not his boat's home.

To me, this home-port thing never seemed like an accurate reflection of a sailor's situation, since living inland often has nothing to do with the place we call home. For me, a landlocked domicile holds about as much warmth and attraction as a cellblock does for an inmate. It's the place where I eat, sleep, and serve my time, but it's not where I live. I "live" on my boat and now my boat is back "home."

For a long time I didn't know where home was, so I was reluctant to paint anything on the sides of *Kontigo* for fear of writing it wrong. I might have preferred to call Green Turtle Cay or Key West my hailing port, but those were merely places of vacation, not my boat's final destination.

This life is not my final destination, either. It's merely a taste of the goodness to come — a place of work, purpose, and relaxation marred by sin. A place where we create meaning and memories before we're called home to the promised land. Madison Avenue would have us believe that we should eat, drink, and be merry — that we should grab all the gusto we can because we only go around once in life. But there is more to life than what we see with our dim eyes. This is not the real thing. Not the final scene. It's only a pale imitation of the glory to come. A dress rehearsal with bad acting and plywood props.

But even a bad play foreshadowing the Broadway performance is better than no play at all. It gives us a sense of place as we're passing through. And so on a warm Sunday afternoon in March, at a small marina along the ICW, I found my home port. We had stopped to get fuel on the final leg of our passage north, and were enjoying the shelter of a small marina as a brisk northwest wind blew down Adams Creek. My friend Pat was commenting on how the hard part of the trip was over — the wet, dark, and cold part. We were enjoying two warm Coronas on a cool spring day among people who spoke with a "high-tider's" accent. The remains of a deli sandwich purchased in Wrightsville Beach provided a simple meal in a marina not recognized for its lavish facilities. It felt special. It felt familiar. It felt like home.

This pause in our passage could never have produced this emotion if I had not pointed *Kontigo* towards the islands that previous fall. Others have said it more eloquently than I, but my heart learned that afternoon that sometimes you have to leave a place to get an accurate accounting of its worth. I had thought that the mud flat where I kept *Kontigo* was just a convenient pause on my way south to more exotic coves and creeks. I didn't know what a home port was until I didn't have one.

But now I do.

If home is where the heart is, then Oriental will always be my home port. Even when I gaze across the shallow coves punctured by patches of coral and volcano outcroppings, I will desire to return to Slip None on the North Dock at Whittaker Creek Yacht Harbor. It's the place where friends look after my boat, toss me a line when I come up the creek, and offer me a cold drink from their icebox — knowing from past experiences that I'm too cheap to buy my own drinks. Home is also the place where I can "borrow" a half can of blue paint to stencil the word "Kontigo" on the hulls of this old trimaran. Painting a name and address on the back of a boat isn't much to brag about, unless you've been without both for a while.

Then it's a big deal indeed.

➤ **Hard Aground hint:** Home is where the heart is, and my heart is home in Oriental.

➤ **Passage markers:** *Do not store up for yourselves treasures on earth, where moth and rust destroy, and where thieves break in and steal. But store up for yourselves treasures in heaven, where moth and rust do not destroy, and where thieves do not break in and steal. For where your treasure is, there your heart will be also.* —Matthew 6:19–21. For further inspiration read Isaiah 40:29–31.

➤ **Prayer focus:** Those seeking their place in the world and a purpose in God's kingdom.

During his morning watch, our captain had extracted a cheap boom box from behind the settee beside the quarter berth, so when I came on duty at noon I had the cockpit, rain, and radio all to myself. I was hoping for an AM station out of Nassau or Cuba, but what I landed instead was just as foreign — at least by some standards. Almost three hundred miles out to sea, where neither bird nor freighter had been sighted for days, I swerved into the Rush Limbaugh Show and another journey into broadcast excellence.

Part V

The Cost of Cruising: Calculating the Coast of Living

26

Oh Say Can You Sea

I was measuring a piece of teak for a rub rail when the husband and wife walked down East Dock. Here in Slip None at Whittaker Creek, the stern of my sailboat points across the creek to a fleet of "Boats for Sale" and I'm always encouraged when anyone stops to consider one of the used boats listed on the brokerage sheet. It's a sign that the country-club culture of the "land-cuffed" lubbers hasn't completely soiled the field for blossoming boaters. This is an important matter since our kind — and by this I mean those of us who cruise — continues to get shoved to the edges of society and locked out of the very harbors to which we flee. By my way of reckoning, the more of us there are the bigger our peace movement and the louder our chant: "Hey, ho, we won't go, and if we go, we go slow!"

As I looked over at the dock, I saw that two small children accompanied the couple. When the father leaned forward to step under the bimini his son followed. The daughter was younger and smaller, more timid than her brother. She stood on the dock staring at the back of her father's floral print shirt until he turned and lifted her across the narrow divide. The mother sat on a dock box, her haunch flattening the white shorts that were absorbing the stains of dock dew. She crossed her ankles and looked at her watch.

"Can you read me the dimensions?" I asked Mason, my youngest son.

"Getting too old to read your handwriting?" he replied.

119

"I've never been able to read my own handwriting, so would you please just read me the dimensions and stop commenting on my poor eyesight?"

He smiled and recited the figures, and as he did I thought how blessed my boys were to have both vigor and vision. Neither son is constricted by the limitations of glasses or contacts, and both seem to have an unbridled amount of energy. I can still surf and snowboard, but lately the small things in life have become something of a blur. The nun and can buoys fall into that category, as does the print for the longitude and latitude on my paper charts. I would like to think this is one of the reasons I stray from the channel so often, but the truth is I was running aground before my eyesight went bad. Reading glasses help, but they haven't improved my navigational abilities. I'm afraid only a hired captain could solve that problem.

"Where's the mom?" I asked, hoping Mason wouldn't notice that I was squinting over the tape measure.

"She's still sitting on the dock box."

"And the dad and kids?"

"They went down below. The boy crawled up through the forward berth and is now leaning back over the hatch, looking down at his sister in the V-berth. I think he's trying to spit on her head."

I grabbed my glasses and marked the wood again. A little vision enhancement makes a big difference when you're struggling to measure a plank of wood or plot a course, but it can also help when trying to focus your family on a vision. Words help, but often the passion of a dream is lost on those focused on the cares of life. Vision is the act of seeing the dream and reaching for it in faith. Nothing is more powerful than an idea whose time has come. Our lives unfold in short cruises that test our resolve. There are ports of prosperity that lead to plenty and test our ability to handle abundance. There are ports of people that bring the unlovely into our lives and strain our capacity to care. There are ports of peril fraught with tragedy that tests our faith in a loving God. And there are ports of temptation that lure us to take what is not ours to have.

Too often I miss the lessons taught in these passages and have to repeat the course. I'm like the land-cuffed tourists who see my boat as just a small ship, but not the home of a family bonded in fellowship by our love of cruising. I'm like the waterfront wanderers who see just a companionway, not the companionship that is nurtured in the close quarters of a warm cabin. When you lack vision you "see" a boat, rather than "sea" the adventures a boat offers.

Too often we sail through life trying to ignore the port of death that's always looming beyond the horizon. But it's out there. Over the rim. If not today, then someday. Life is not about arriving. It's about the people who sail with us on the passage.

Jesus tells of a certain rich man whose business prospered. The man thought to himself, "What shall I do? I have no place to store my crops." So he said, "I will tear down my barns and build bigger ones, and there I will store all my grain and my goods. And I'll say to myself, 'You have plenty of good things laid up for many years. Take life easy; eat, drink and be merry.' But God said to him, 'You fool! This very night your life will be demanded from you. Then who will get what you have prepared for yourself?'"

We can't take it with us. The only thing that remains is the legacy of how we loved others and loved God. As parents, we can teach our children to trust in education, hard work, and themselves, but if we neglect to teach them to trust in the Lord, we fail them. Sometimes cruising is the best way to teach that lesson. Other times, it is not. We each have to discover the best classroom for training up a child, and I've found a boat is a good lab for the coursework. That's why my son was with me that morning. We were cutting wood and shaping his character.

I marked the plank of teak with a dull pencil and then fired up the circular saw.

"What's the mom doing now?" I asked.

"Standing on the dock with her arms folded."

"And the husband?"

"He's back in the cockpit showing his son how to adjust the main sheet traveler. The little girl just got off the boat."

"That's not good."

"What, that the girl got off the boat?"

"No, this board I cut. It's an inch too short. How'd that happen?"

"Because you didn't let me do it. I told you those reading glasses wouldn't help. Here, let me try."

When I sat back in the cockpit I saw that the man and his son were stepping off the boat. I watched as the father stood for a moment, clutching the hand of his boy. He looked to be studying the rigging and mentally calculating the replacement costs of hardware, sails, and wiring. Wondering, I suppose, if the boat would be worth the trouble. If he had asked, I would have told him that it was, but he wasn't asking.

His wife began to walk back towards their minivan, tugging at the hand of her daughter. Leaving her husband to dream his dream alone. Turning her back on their future together as he dreamed of the two of them looking west towards a sun setting over the Sea of Abaco. Their backs braced against cockpit cushions, his hand resting in hers. Sniffing the smell of fresh coffee as they motored south from Georgetown on a cold November morning. Laughing with their children as they dove off the swim ladder on Christmas Day in the Keys. Nestled together under a starlit sky, his hand stroking the tanned flanks of her shoulder.

All she'd see was a childish man standing on an old boat who refused to spend time on the real things in life like career advancement, yard work, and home repairs. Why couldn't he see how hard she worked to balance the checkbook? Why couldn't he see how tough it was to get the kids to soccer practice and how tired she was in the evenings? Why didn't he notice how the two of them never had time for slow walks, long conversations, and the tender clutch of spent affection? Worst of all why didn't he care that she was stressed all the time from trying to hold it all together?

What she didn't know then, but would find out later, was that he did care, had cared and always would. And she would know that for certain in the coming months. She just needed to "sea" his love from my perspective.

➤ **Hard Aground hint:** In God's eyes we're all a success waiting to happen. We just need to take that first step and move forward.

➤ **Passage markers:** *Praise the Lord, O my soul . . . who satisfies your desires with good things so that your youth is renewed like the eagle's.* —Psalm 103:1, 5. For further guidance read Joshua 1:5–9.

➤ **Prayer focus:** Couples struggling to adjust to a diverse set of dreams.

27

Knock on Wood

THE MORNING AFTER BOB DEATON'S FUNERAL I AWOKE TO FIND A red-headed woodpecker of some dark denomination drilling a hole in the top of my dock piling. Pecking away in the bright sunlight. Knocking on wood. Reminding me that I should be too.

The bird departed when I lifted the top hatch board of my sailboat and stepped into the cockpit, disturbing the glaze of frost that coated the cushions. I looped a leg over the lifeline, found good footing on the narrow pad along the toe rail, and stepped onto the finger pier. My yard-sale bike, a boy's model at least two generations too small for my short legs, was propped against the white dock box. The black seat was gray under the dusting of frozen dew. The air was cold. Mighty cold. Too cold for me to be riding a bike on a narrow dock in February.

I mounted the bike, pointed the front tire south, and started towards the bathhouse, hoping this would be one of those good mornings when the hot water heater worked. The apparent wind from my forward progress bit into my thin skin, but I didn't risk adjusting my grip for fear of veering off the dock and into the creek. I'd tested the temperature of the water in February, once, clothed only in jeans and sneakers. It wasn't an experience I wanted to repeat.

So I rode slowly, shifting the small pouch of shower garb over the front spokes, centering the weight more evenly, making careful corrections to keep me in the center of the dock. The sun was rising over the black pine tops. Dock lines glistened like tinsel as sunlight broke through. Hot breath formed dense clouds as I worked the low gear. Beneath my pedals I could see fresh tire tracks carving a slender trail in the thick icing on the planks.

There was a lot of beauty in the early hours of that cold February morning, but it came with some pain. Thin air burned my lungs. Knuckles hurt from the chilled wind. Eyes watered from the intense cold. Pleasure and pain were both a part of the morning. You can't have the splendor of a winter sunrise frozen in time without the pain of the cold. The sting of death mutes the joy of life, and it's a very gray world indeed, without both.

The hot water worked, but the pressure was low. I hurried along, changed into my author's outfit and headed for New Bern to participate in the first annual Book Lovers Affair. Skip Crayton was there promoting his book, *Remember When*. My cousin Carolyn Booth was giving away home-baked cookies and selling copies of *Aunt Mag's Recipe Book*. I set my box down on the short end of a long table, saving most of the counter space for Nicholas Sparks. I knew Sparks would have more books to sell, knew he probably hadn't reserved space at the event, and knew too he probably wasn't coming. If Sparks did show up then maybe he'd appreciate my generosity and offer a word of advice for how to become a best-selling author. Most likely he'd say, "Write." All successful writers say the same thing: "Just write." For a crowd that claims to be creative, writers can be a dull lot sometimes.

Sparks didn't arrive, but Ben Casey did, so I shared my space with Ben. He sold a few books, smiled for the women who took his picture, and then left early to eat lunch with his wife. Ben was good company. His fellowship made the slow day move faster.

But there remained a chill in the air. A tremor of remorse rattled the crowd whenever the conversation turned to Oriental and boating. The news was still too fresh, the after shocks too close to home. Someone would stop to look at the cover of my book, tell their own story of how they'd run aground, and then end with, "It's just awful about Bob's death, isn't it?"

It was. And it is. And it will be for sometime. Fifty-two was a good-sized number, but it's not big enough. Not by a long shot.

The great deception of life is to believe that we'll live for a very long time, that we'll always have another chance to make a difference. But we won't. Often we only get one chance to do the right thing, at the right time, for the wrong kind of person — for the person who is interrupting our plans with their own petty problems. Then we're off again on our bike or car or boat filling another busy moment with ourselves. Making a living, making a life, making excuses for why we can't stop to help or hear or offer a measure of hope to someone in need.

I missed Bob's funeral. I didn't think I knew him well enough to attend. But I should have gone. I should have gone out of respect for his life, out of respect for what he meant to this community. I should have gone to testify that his life made a difference, that his work had meaning, was necessary and good. It would have only taken a little time out of my day. I had the time.

I should have spent some.

➢ **Hard Aground hint:** Time is the only contraband we bring into this world, and what we don't spend on others we should exchange for memories.

➢ **Passage markers:** *Jesus called in a loud voice, "Lazarus, come out!" The dead man came out, his hands and feet wrapped with strips of linen, and a cloth around his face. Jesus said to them, "Take off the grave clothes and let him go."* —John 11:43–44. For further guidance read Ecclesiastes 3:1–8.

➢ **Prayer focus:** Those tempted to spend more time on things than people.

28

May I Mayreau?

THE ATLANTIC WAS COBALT BLUE AND CRUSTY WITH CRUMBS OF WHITE foam the morning after Pam agreed to marry Dan. An easterly breeze was blowing across the short sand spit that separated Salt Whistle Bay from the Tobago Cays, and it was a welcome visitor in the forward bunk drenched in stale sweat and morning breath.

"You think I'd leave your side?" Dan asked, rolling over to study the tanned flanks of his bride-to-be. "You know me better than that."

She responded with a deep inhalation between her petite snores. "You think I'd leave you when you are down on your knees hurling over the side?" he asked, not expecting an answer. "I wouldn't do that." He tilted his head and kissed the pink patch of sun-ripened meat on her right shoulder, then extracted himself from the V-berth to prepare his mermaid a cup of coffee.

The act was a simple task that would in no way reflect the gratitude and relief Dan felt on this first morning of his matrimony-to-be. Dan and his coffee were like the widow and her mite on the steps of the Temple — small and insignificant, seen only by those who knew the heart of the matter. An elaborate meal of fresh fruits, bacon, and toast would have been a more elegant offering, but Dan's small sacrifice of coffee was all he could muster this day. He was too "bottle fatigued" to do more.

The debris of the engagement party lay scattered among the pots and plates stacked on the counter beside the sink. With the blunt edge of a greasy

127

butter knife Dan pried at the hardened noodles bonded to the burners of the CNG stove. The previous evening had been unbearably hot in the galley and no one, least of all Dan, had wanted to remain below scrubbing away stray noodles and spaghetti sauce when good wine and steady winds flowed freely on deck. He would clean it later, he had told himself, and now it was later.

Cracker crumbs, a wine glass, and at least one member of his crew — the crew he could see but not hear, were wedged in the cushions of the settee. The louder members of his engagement entourage had slept on deck as a courtesy to the rest of the crew. These few but strong slumbered in the cockpit, dispensing the thunder of their bedtime bellows downwind onto the rest of the fleet in Mayreau.

Dan polished a patch of countertop with dish detergent until he had a small but clean pad on which to place the two coffee mugs — the two he had packed just for this occasion. "To my pirate, with love" said Pam's cup to Dan. "To my mermaid, with love" said his to her. Dan pressed the gas button on the stove and waited for the flame to build. This would be a special brew made with Brazilian beans purchased from a small boy on Canouan. The beans had been ground by Dan's own hands, each cupful measured out with love. The blend would be stronger than any Starbucks flavor of the week, and the aroma would stir Pam from her slumber with the magic of a morning kiss. Like a ray of sunshine spreading across the Atlantic with the passing of a tropical shower, Dan had seen this morning coming from a long way off.

But there was a cloud on his face. Dan released the CNG switch and stepped away from the cold burner. Someone, perhaps himself, he thought, must've closed the gas valve before they went to bed. He was surprised to realize that he could have thought so clearly after the night's festivities, but it made him feel smart to think he had remembered to turn off the gas. Clear thinking would come in handy when he and Pam were cruising these islands alone.

When he looked under the sink he saw that the valve was open so he pressed the switch again and waited. "It would be just my luck to run out of gas on this, of all mornings," Dan thought as he stared at the black coil on the stove, wishing the gas tanks were somewhere other than in the lazaret under a crew member. Dan knew as soon as he asked one body to move, they would all stir, and the silent magic of the moment would be lost.

In the States, there's a Starbucks on every corner, but islands don't have corners, so Dan looked through the portal beyond his own boat towards the other vessel in his engagement armada. He could see the white shape of a coffee mug resting on the combing of the cockpit and he thanked God for neighborly neighbors who brewed coffee before sunrise. Dan gathered the two prenuptial cups and his coffee fixings and stepped off the swim platform and into his dinghy.

When I saw Dan approaching, working the oars of his inflatable instead of the throttle on the handle, I figured he was suffering from outboard problems again, so I asked if he needed gas or a fresh spark plug.

"No, the motor's running fine. I just didn't want to wake my crew," he said, looping the painter around my stern cleat. "Can I get some coffee?"

My brew was cheap and a little strong with a slightly burned flavor, but once Dan added the whipped cream and nutmeg it looked like a $2.75 cup of something special. He said thanks for the coffee and, like everything Dan does, including his offer to wed for life, he meant it with all his heart. I watched Dan as he paddled away, leaning into the easterly breeze as he pulled at the oars. When he reached his boat, he stepped around the snoring members of his crew and carefully climbed down the companionway to deliver Pam her coffee in bed.

There are other ways to say "I love you," and Dan's simple act will never match the sacrifice of a widow's mite in the Gospel of Luke, but on a windy morning in Salt Whistle Bay, on the island of Mayreau, Dan demonstrated to anyone willing to watch, what true love looked like. I watched and wished I cherished my wife like that. I do not know if Pam enjoyed her cup of slightly burned coffee, but I have no doubt that Dan enjoyed the act of giving.

The aroma of love has that flavor about it.

➤ **Hard Aground hint:** You can give without loving, but you can't love without giving. Sometimes just showing up for the passage is a gift of love.

➤ **Passage markers:** *In this same way, husbands ought to love their wives as their own bodies. He who loves his wife loves himself.* —Ephesians 5:28. For further guidance read Genesis 2:18–25.

➤ **Prayer focus:** Those trying to fill the emptiness in their heart with something other than the love of God and the mate he's provided.

29

Recharging My Batteries

MY SISTER MARJI, THE ONE WHO SPENDS HER VACATIONS SAILING AROUND the British Virgin Islands on any boat that'll float, asked me this week what I wanted for my birthday. I told her I wanted the same thing this year that I wanted last year and every year I could remember since college. I wanted to be in the islands with a pair of salt-stained leather sandals anchoring my tanned feet to the deck of an old sailboat. She said she couldn't get me to the islands this spring, but she could get me the new Jimmy Buffett CD, which, in her view, was the next best thing.

Ah, if only that were true.

There was a time, back in the 1970s, when listening to Fingers Taylor introduce the opening stanza of "A Pirate Looks at Forty" could transport me to the islands. But like Peter Pan and Captain Hook, Buffett grew up and so did his music. Now when I hear an old Buffett tune I'm reminded that the tan lines above my ankles are evidence that too many domestic duties and degrees in latitude separate me from the islands Buffett used to write and sing about.

I told my sister she could keep the CD. I told her what I really wanted was to sail my boat to Cape Lookout, or Ocracoke, or Charleston because sailing to any of those places would be way more fun than listening to some rich and famous relic from the Gulf Coast sing about a time when he was passionate and poor. She told me I was an old fart, which I am. Too many birthdays will make you one, but an abundance of birthdays is better than the alternative. Besides, when I'm in the mood for a festive evening that features boats, beaches, and bars, I slip the dock lines and sail to Beaufort where the Dockhouse provides the perfect venue for savoring the simple sounds of an outdoor concert.

When the breeze is stiff, but not a gale, and the no-see-ums are hiding in the low-tide flats on Carrot Island, I can lie on a cockpit cushion past midnight listening to the sounds of a blue-collar band working up the crowd on Front Street. When the evening mist coats me with a tacky texture of salt-laden dew, I retreat to the stale heat of my cabin and let the swells in Taylor's Creek rock me to sleep as the music flows across the anchorage. On nights like this when there's still ice in the cooler and the drinks are cold, I have the best seat in the house — house being a generous term for the description of any boat I've owned. It's a cheap way to recharge my batteries and a lot more fun than standing in a football stadium with a crowd of drunk college kids singing "Margaritaville" who aren't even old enough to buy tequila.

Sometimes I don't even have to leave the dock to catch a live performance. Back when we used to moor my Ranger 33 in the middle of Whittaker Creek, Bennie and I would sit in the cockpit and track the stars and satellites across the northern sky while some fellow up the creek practiced his saxophone. Normally a practicing musician with a loud horn is about as lethal as a practicing attorney with a class-action suit, but this guy was closer to perfection than practicing. Beneath a star-speckled sky on a cool evening, Bennie and I would share all the romance we could stand on a boat constrained by two small boys slumbering in the V-berth. Bennie would nuzzle her cheek against my chest and we would talk of all the places that *Walter Mitty* would take us. It doesn't matter now that *Walter Mitty* never made it to all those islands. As with so many things in life, the passage and people made the journey fun — even on the nights when we never left port.

A few years later, though, it was the port that made the performance memorable. We were anchored in Black Sound on Green Turtle Cay, straining to hear the Gully Roosters above the drone of the town's power plant. Rumbling bass notes competed with the constant hum of the diesel generator, and every few minutes we'd hear Kevin McIntosh singing "Sandra, My Love." The quality of the acoustics wasn't much better than a Buffett concert in a basketball arena, but I can still hear the sounds of the Abacos ringing in my ears.

Recently I enjoyed a raucous evening at anchor in Grenada listening to a band perform at the Sunset Bar and Restaurant. Sitting on the lower lip of the swim platform, warming my feet in the Caribbean Sea, I'm certain that was the best Soca music ever played.

Music is therapy for the soul. The major and minor chords strum the strings of my heart in ways words never can. The notes speak a language that refreshes our spirit when tough times press in upon us. Whenever I hear a song promising rest and relaxation in a paradise of salt and sun, my spirit soars. It reminds me that this planet, as wonderful as it may be, is not my home. That beyond the last breath, there is a paradise I've never seen that is free of pain, sorrow, and disappointments. It is a place wide and wild, filled with hidden treasures just waiting to be explored.

The call of paradise that tugs at my heart reflects my deep desire to return to Eden, to be reunited with the God who created us and all that is good in creation. Far too often we search for the ecstasy of Eden through fabricated pharmaceuticals that leave us dull and dopey. We swap friendships with slip-mates because we think the next date will be our Adam or Eve, but they never are. We have been kicked out of the garden and left to roam the earth longing for a way back up that river to the perfect port.

Jesus said, "Do not let your hearts be troubled. Trust in God; trust also in me. In my Father's house are many rooms; if it were not so, I would have told you. I am going there to prepare a place for you. And if I go and prepare a place for you, I will come back and take you to be with me that you also may be where I am." When I hear the call of paradise in the music of the islands it reminds me that there is a promised land. A unique and perfect place for each of use. A room with a view and enough Son to warm me forever.

So I explained to my sister that what I really wanted for my birthday was a generator for my boat because with the heat and humidity soaking my shorts in summer sweat, I needed the extra juice to keep the cabin cool, the drinks cold, and my radio playing this new Buffett CD. I mean, let's face it. Even a bad day on the water with bare feet and Buffett is better than any day on land in sneakers and socks.

➤ **Hard Aground hint:** Outwardly we are wasting away, but inwardly we are renewed each day by the Spirit of Christ.

➤ **Passage markers:** *I come that they might have life, and have it to the full.* —John 10:10. For further guidance read Psalm 33.

➤ **Prayer focus:** The Peter-Pan parents of children and grandchildren still searching for Margaritaville.

30

Diving for Pennies

SOMEWHERE ALONG THE WAY I BLEW IT. AS I SAT IN THE COCKPIT reading Dave and Carolyn's letter from the Bahamas, I realized that sometime over the past thirty years my plans for world cruising have veered drastically off course. I don't know if it was a series of bad fixes, the fact that I can't plot a course too well, or some peculiar social current that's whisked me into the mainstream of life, but the fact is, I'm lost and scared.

I know some enjoy the security of steady employment interrupted by frenzied weekends of short cruises, but I'm not one of these people. I tend to lurch to extremes in search of adventure and meaning, and this current course I'm on is not how I'd hoped to spend my youth — youth being any age preceding rigor mortis. If I was going to be chained to anything at this stage in my life it was to a firm sandy bottom in a cove near some far-flung tropical island beyond the reach of the evening news, the IRS, and this impatient editor of mine. If my friends wanted to find me they were going to need the assistance of the Bahamas Air Sea Rescue Association because I had every intention of sailing over the edge. I had a plan. A good one too. Leave it to my best friend to mess it up.

It was June, sometime during the Carter administration, and I'd just graduated from NC State with a degree in English. The journalism aspect of my degree had allowed me to write for the *Technician,* State's campus newspaper, and it was during my time on the paper that I was assigned the task of covering a concert by Jimmy Buffett, a fledgling musician working the local college scene. While others at the event became intoxicated on cheap beer and pot, I merely became infected with the casual Caribbean lifestyle Buffett claimed to have found in the lower latitudes.

That summer I convinced my best friend that we should fly to the Bahamas to spend the next few years sailing the Out Islands and surfing the best reef breaks. He was too stupid to know I was serious, so he said yes, and we bought tickets on an Eastern Air Lines flight for Nassau. "Come Monday" became our theme song and Coppertone our cologne. I wasn't about to tell anyone where I was going — certainly not my girlfriend and future wife. I figured my plan would seem stupid and reckless in her eyes, which it was, so there was no point in debating an argument I'd already lost. Better to just keep my mouth shut and send her a post card from Eleuthera.

Well, wouldn't you know the day before we were set to depart, my buddy got a call from the convenience store asking if he was still interested in working the graveyard shift. Apparently the previous night clerk was slow to respond to the phrase "Give me all your money" and there was a sudden vacancy. They didn't tell Kevin this, of course. And he didn't tell me he'd taken the job until I arrived at his home that Monday to drive us to the airport. He said it wasn't a permanent gig, just a temporary assignment to help him catch up on some past bills, but the job lasted long enough to ruin my dreams of an endless summer.

I never told Bennie how close I came to attaining fugitive status and so, despite her parents' objections, she married me the next spring. Or maybe it was the spring after that. When you've been incarcerated in martial bliss as long as we have, the years run together. Within a few months I assumed a mortgage, and the elusive endless summer slipped further away until it became nothing more than a tired old tale of my missed youth. I guess that's why Dave and Carolyn's letter tugged at my heart so. It was a reminder that they were living the endless summer I never had.

It's hard to look back and ponder what might have been. It's hard to give up a dream, but a dream that doesn't die cannot be revived. There can't be a resurrection without a corpse — and my soul died a little that Monday when I

backed out of Kevin's driveway and returned home.

But I see it rising from the dead in the hearts of my boys. My oldest son, Win, plans to cross the Pacific this summer to spend a year studying in Australia and surfing the best reef breaks in Bali. If he needs crew, I'll be ready to help, but if he decides to sail with friends that'll be okay too.

My youngest son, Mason, just returned from Utah, where he stood on a mountaintop with a snowboard strapped to his feet, feeling the breath of God in his face as he dropped into a bowl of fresh snow. Both have their own endless dreams, dreams that were nurtured because I was willing to let mine go, marry their mother, and foster a family. I may not have memories of that endless summer but I have so much more.

So if you're cruising the Bahamas this winter and see Dave and Carolyn feasting on cracked conch and fresh grouper as a peppercorn sky sets over Nassau, tell them I said hello. Tell them I'm still diving for pennies in the pool instead of lobster on the reef, because somewhere along the way I blew it. Or rather, it blew me away. And it blows me away still.

➤ **Hard Aground hint:** Some are called to greatness and some are called to serve. I'm called "Dad" and that's fine with me.

➤ **Passage markers:** *Now to him who is able to do immeasurably more than all we ask or imagine, according to his power that is at work within us, to him be the glory.* —Ephesians 3:20–21. For further guidance read I Kings 18:43–44.

➤ **Prayer focus:** Men trying to father boys.

31

Happy Daddy's Day

WE WERE TWO DAYS OUT OF BEAUFORT, NORTH CAROLINA, AND SOME three hundred miles south and east of Cape Hatteras, rollicking along on a wild, lumpy sea on the fringes of a nor'easter that was pausing, not passing as predicted. Despite the low-slung storm clouds that framed the northwestern sky, the wind, waves, and boat were all moving towards the same tropical latitudes, so we weren't concerned with the growing gale — only thankful for the ride and the simple perfection of a self-steering wind vane. We had exhausted our stock of recreational diversions the first day out, so our crew had resorted to bawdy pranks with hot dogs and the Polaroid camera. Pity the poor crew member who slept in the salon.

During his morning watch, our captain had extracted a cheap boom box from behind the settee beside the quarter berth, so when I came on duty at noon I had the cockpit, rain, and radio all to myself. I was hoping for an AM station out of Nassau or Cuba, but what I landed instead was just as foreign — at least by some standards. Almost three hundred miles out to sea, where neither bird nor freighter had been sighted for days, I swerved into the Rush Limbaugh Show and another journey into broadcast excellence. Limbaugh was almost humble that day, speaking of the pride his father had felt when his son "Rusty" had finally achieved national prominence as a talk show host. The afternoon discussion centered on callers sharing their own desire for their father's approval and the importance dads make in the lives of their children.

My father never cared for Limbaugh and he never cared for sailing. Dad was a motorboat man with a special affection for outboards that were in disrepair. To my knowledge, Dad never had an outboard motor that ran for an entire afternoon, but that never stopped him from taking a chance on an overused, underserviced Johnson. Those hot, windless days we spent on the water watching Dad tinker on his outboard helped to plant within me a love for the sea that not even trash in a carburetor can kill.

When I was eight years old I was sure my father was the greatest man alive. He was a tall, lanky fellow with shoulders so broad he could carry me around like a lightweight jacket. On his days off he would take me camping in the Smoky Mountains or haul me down to the coast. He taught me to bait my own hook, and when he thought I was a pretty fair fisherman, he took me to the Pamlico River where I caught twenty-six fish in a single afternoon. It wasn't until many years later that I learned I'd been catching the same tired fish all day as Dad snuck the wounded soldier off the dock and reattached him to my hook. Dad believed you could give a boy a fish and feed him for a day, or teach a boy to fish and keep him occupied for a weekend.

Dad tried hard to make me a fisherman. He'd take me out of school when the spots were running, and we'd share a small tent on Topsail Island with a squadron of mosquitoes and no-see-ums. Early in the morning, as the sun erupted beneath the horizon, we'd cast our lines past the breakers and into a school tearing at the water. That evening I'd haul my sleeping bag onto the pier to nap at the heels of my father. Dad wasn't the best fisherman ever to live, but he sure loved to fish and while I never learned to love fishing the way Dad did, I always loved fishing with him.

Dad laughed a lot back then and was inclined to build anything I wanted out of scrap plywood and two-by-fours. He built a motorboat one summer from a set of plans he found in a *Popular Mechanics* magazine. Mom kept yelling at him from the upstairs window to clean up the mess, but Dad wasn't easily discouraged, so within a few weeks we had a fine plywood motorboat.

In the scheme of life a home-built motorboat is not much of an accomplishment, but when you're eight years old and enamored with the strength and wisdom of your father's abilities, it's a big deal. On the day we launched that boat and watched it float off the trailer, I decided my dad was just short of divine. I don't remember much else about the boat except that it developed a case of rot and had to be cut up and hauled off. Of course, by then I was a teenager and Dad wasn't as tall or wise.

He got another motorboat, but the outings weren't as much fun. Dad would launch the boat while the rest of us hauled our gear down to the campsite. The outboard always started on the second pull because Dad worked on motors the way Limbaugh works on liberals — it was a passion with him. We'd get a little ways from shore, then throttle up and go roaring off in a puff of smoke. On a good day, we'd get a hundred yards away from shore before the motor would quit.

On a bad day, we'd get a mile out.

If it was one of those good, hundred-yard days, my sister and I would jump in with our life jackets and swim back to camp, leaving dad to tinker with an outboard that ran only in the metal barrel out back of our garage. It was during this phase of my youth that I learned to loathe motorboats.

Dad doesn't own a boat anymore and he doesn't fish much either. He says they don't bite like they used to, and he's proved it by not wetting a hook in more than five years. He doesn't like sailboats, and he doesn't like Limbaugh, and he doesn't like the idea of his son dodging tropical storms out in the Atlantic. Dad likes his satellite dish and his cable box, and he likes hearing from his boy when I'm safely back on land. But I believe that afternoon on our way to the Bahamas even Dad would have enjoyed fishing with his son one last time.

I was coming off watch and searching the icebox for dinner, when the trolling line sang out in that octave that lets you know it's a big one. I closed the lid and ran on deck to help reduce sail and slow the boat. There may be plenty of fish in the ocean, but nobody likes losing one when you're hungry, and we were too thrilled with the prospect of fresh seafood to toy with that fish. We gaffed him and killed him and let the yellowfin tuna soak in lemon while we celebrated our catch with a round of drinks. I can't remember the last time a fish tasted that good. Dad would have loved it.

So here's to Dad and fathers everywhere, both in heaven and on earth, who push us to find our passion and explore the potential that lies within us. Happy Daddy's Day, Dad. I miss you.

➤ **Hard Aground hint:** To father a child is easy. It's growing into the title that consumes your life and makes you worthy of the name.

➤ **Passage markers:** *Train a child in the way he should go, and when he is old he will not turn from it.* —Proverbs 22:6. For further guidance read 2 Corinthians 1:3–7.

➤ **Prayer focus:** Children who need encouragement and parents who need the wisdom to guide them.

32

The Cost of Cruising

IT WAS NOT THE HAPPIEST DAY OF MY LIFE, AS MANY HAD CLAIMED it would be, but there was a peace in my heart as we stepped off our boat and onto the dock that final time. *Walter Mitty* had been sold — pawned off to be exact — and we were out from under the burden of caring for an old sailboat. Lest anyone try to convince you otherwise, boat ownership is a stout obligation that can drive even the strongest man to tears. It did me.

Our painful journey down this path of broken dreams began the weekend I sheared off a stud on the block of my Atomic Four gasoline engine and shackled my crew to the dock for an extended holiday weekend. While other families sailed to Cape Lookout, Beaufort, and Ocracoke, we immersed ourselves in communal sweat and tried to pacify the cranky beast that lived beneath the cockpit steps. The thermostat was stuck shut, restricting the flow of cool water that normally surged through the intestines of the beast. In an act of desperation and self-reliance, I'd commandeered a thermostat off an abandoned Ford pickup truck, and I was certain the whole project wouldn't take more than an hour. At least, that's what I told the family. We'd be late for the raft-up at Cape Lookout and probably miss the hors d'oeuvres on *Red Baron,* but it was the Fourth of July, and as long as we arrived in time for the sunset and fireworks, what did it matter?

I extracted the first three bolts with ease, but that's always the way it is in these matters. That Atomic Four engine was like a big-league baseball pitcher,

143

enticing me with fast pitches low and away, hoping to nail me in the ear with a high, fast one. I'm speaking figuratively here, but the baseball analogy works, because when I tried to remove the last bolt, I found the threads of the nut woven into the stud like pinstripes in a Yankee uniform. There was just no way I was going to remove that nut with a box-end wrench.

I hopped in my dinghy and paddled across the creek to Sailcraft, where I hoped to borrow a stud remover. Loaning out tools to incompetent boat owners was against the boatyard's policy, but I knew the owner and he felt sorry for me. I also suspect he saw some mechanical work coming his way, since there was very little chance I would use the tool properly and thus, I was likely to destroy what was otherwise a good engine. I returned to my boat with the stud remover and began to pull and tap, stopping every few minutes to squirt WD-40 all over the motor and my forearms. Finally the nut broke free — but not in one piece. The part that was joined to the stud remained stuck. And now, so were we.

A lot of broken dreams fused together in that heated moment. That was not the first time I'd been disappointed by *Walter Mitty*'s temperamental mood swings, and it would certainly not be the last. But it was a turning point. From that moment on, the charm of boat ownership was gone. The concept of weekend cruising changed from joy to job, and I realized how ill-prepared I was for the task. I remember looking up at Bennie through angry eyes filled with perspiration and tears, demanding to know why anyone would spend good time and money for this sort of misery.

"Surely, camping in a stand of pines at the base of Cape Lookout with a bevy of sand fleas gnawing at the canals in my nostrils can't be any worse than this," I said. "Why'd you let me talk you into buying this boat?"

"Because I love you and thought it would make you happy."

"Well, it didn't. So don't be so nice next time, okay?"

"You mean there's going to be a next time?"

It's not important to know how we stumbled into a 33-foot sailboat, or why we agreed to commit to something of that magnitude without first considering the implications of big-boat ownership. It's only enough to know that we had agreed to finance and care for *Walter Mitty* until the mortgage was retired or death or bankruptcy forced its sale. That weekend we had finally done our part. We were dead broke and my dreams were bankrupt.

There are costs involved with any boat, no matter if it's a Hobie or a Hinckley, and you're always going to spend more than you'd planned. After I stepped off the boat that final time and tucked the broker's check into my jeans pocket, I decided I would try to calculate the cost of cruising. I tabulated all our expenses, including groceries, fuel, slip fees, yard bills, and insurance to arrive at a total that would provide a rough formula for projecting the cost of cruising. I admit the formula is not very scientific, but then neither is love and that seems to work pretty well — or at least it did until I began to take my wife sailing.

When I tried to calculate the cost of cruising I found that I could get the approximate annual outlay by taking the general market value of our boat and multiplying that figure by fifteen percent. In our case we had a twenty-thousand-dollar boat that cost us around three thousand dollars a year to maintain. Our yearly mortgage payment was about the same. So for around six thousand dollars a year we had access to a thirty-year-old boat that we used about once a month. When viewed like this cruising seemed like a bad investment. What no formula can calculate, however, is the value of those boating memories.

How do you place a price on a sunrise stroll along Masonboro Island as gulls tear at a school of fish feeding in the surf? How do you gauge the value of an afternoon spent surfing a solitary beach break at Shackleford Banks, or measure the wonder of wild ponies grazing on your path as you hike back across the dunes? How can you calculate the cost of playing king-of-the-dinghy with boys too young to know the difference between a twenty-dollar beach raft and a two-thousand-dollar inflatable boat? When you're eight or five, or eighty-five, who's to say what you'll pay for that moment then?

As they strap you onto the silver tray of a hospital gurney and wheel you into the emergency room, who's to say what memories will comfort you then? Maybe the rusty remembrance of a sunset dipping behind the sand dunes will bring a slight smile to your face as the morphine drip sooths the pain. What would you pay for those cruising memories then?

When my boys are grown and gone, will they remember the predictable pirate stories I spun on the bow as we looked up at starlit skies? Will they sit in traffic years from now and yearn for another slow walk along the sandy lanes of Ocracoke Island? Will they ever eat spaghetti again and not recall the loony antics of their parents dancing on the bow to Buffett as a summer squall scrubbed them clean of the homework and yard work and all the work that comes with growing up? Who can say what that memory will be worth then?

During our final voyage on *Walter Mitty* we joined our friends Joe and Debbie in the Bight at Cape Lookout for the last long weekend of the summer. Between the two boats we had one skinny chicken, a bottle of screw-top wine, and a Ziploc bag of dirty rice. On its own it didn't look like much, but between friends on a cruise, it was a feast. The girls seasoned everything generously with garlic and spices, and Joe allowed it all to roast slowly over the embers of our small charcoal grill. The aroma lingered in the cockpit, filling the boat with the smells of festive eating. It was then, between the tears of laughter and calls for seconds, that we turned our eyes westward towards a sun melting into the dunes.

"Just look at that," Joe said reaching over to take Debbie's hand. "This is what life's all about right here. It doesn't get any better than this."

He was right, of course. Whenever hearts and dreams are added to the equation, the cost of cruising can never be measured in purely economic terms. Thank God, life is more precious than that.

In fact, it's priceless.

➤ **Hard Aground hint:** "Don't ask yourself what the world needs. Ask yourself what makes you come alive and do that, because what the world needs is people who have come alive." —HAROLD WHITMAN

➤ **Passage markers:** *Each of you should look not only to your own interests, but also to the interests of others.* —Philippians 2:4. For further guidance read Luke 14:28–35.

➤ **Prayer focus:** Those who need to embrace the people in their life and the adventure God is calling them towards.

Epilogue

A Prayer to Follow Jesus

As the deer pants for streams of water,
so my soul pants for you, O God.
My soul thirsts for God, the living God . . .
Deep calls to deep
in the roar of your waterfalls;
all your waves and breakers
have swept over me.

Psalm 42:1–2, 7

O GOD, WHO CREATED THE EARTH AND SKY, AND THE MAJESTIC WATERS
that have captured my heart and caught my imagination:.

For long seasons of my life I have sensed you in the midst
of Your creation, but I could not find You fully nor give Your face a name.

And so the best that I could do was to feel You as the breeze cooled my skin,
Hear You as the water sloshed beneath my boat,
See You as the waves kicked high and sparkled toward Your sun.

But the waves and the sun were mere hints of what was to come,
As Your face now has a name for me through the One — a Son — Jesus.

I have heard his message of love and acceptance, hope and peace.
And the thirst for the sea has now turned to a thirst for the living water of Jesus.

O God, I'm new at this journey, and I'm not quite sure how to begin.
I can only be real and lay it all on your table of grace,
Bringing to You all the broken, failed, in-need-of repair pieces of my life.

So hear my confession and admission of my sin this day,
And forgive me for the years I've wasted looking for You only by the water.

For You have been above me, beneath me, beside me, and around me,
Everywhere my journey of life has taken me.

And now I ask that You come within me,
As Savior and Deliverer from all that I have become and have been,
Enabling me to live a life of selfless giving that Jesus modeled on his cross.

Change me permanently, deep within,
Far beyond the temporary lifting of my soul during those brief moments upon the seas.

Something is now different, and I don't want to be the same person I was before,
Clinging to the ways that have brought me defeat, despair, disappointment and,
at times, death.

Now You, O God, have captured my heart,
Caught my imagination,
And I now unashamedly determine that with Your help, I will follow Jesus.

Amen.

Dr. Gregory P. Rogers
Pastor, Oakmont Baptist Church
Greenville, North Carolina

▷ ▷ ▷